What If...?

The Architecture and Design of David Rockwell

With contributions by
Justin Davidson
Elizabeth Diller
John Guare
Jack O'Brien

Edited by Chee Pearlman

Metropolis Books

What if an architect could be as experimental as a chef?

What if nature told you what to do?  What if a boutique hotel took a drive down Route 66?  What if the bellhop was a robot?  What if your environment transformed with every step?  What if the

biggest show on earth was

the most intimate one?

What if the set became a

character?  What if a

restaurant could vanish at a

moment's notice?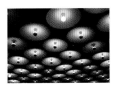

What if you made playgrounds

portable, and kids could ask,

"What if...?"

Preface

Chee Pearlman

What if an architect tirelessly questioned what is?

David Rockwell has spent 30 years forging a practice built on asking exactly that: What if…? What if an architect worked at the intersection of theater, craft, and design? What if he could convince his clients to help him redraw the boundaries of his own profession?

To march a 150-person firm to the drumbeat of "What if…?" is to stay open to the widest range of ideas. Rockwell's secret is to lead with optimism, a strategy that embraces challenges as opportunities. A case in point: The recent commission for a new TED conference theater in Vancouver, British Columbia, exploded into a flurry of "what ifs" focused on a single purpose—make 1,200 people feel as if each one of them has the best seat in the house.

Rockwell asked: What if both intimacy and grandeur could be felt in the same theater? What if every person could be no more than 80 feet from the speaker on the stage? What if there were 16 different kinds of seating—from couches to lounges to desk chairs—to try out during the five-day gathering of TED? Oh, and what if the 20,000-square-foot-structure had to be demountable and storable—disassembled within 72 hours and set up each year in less than 120 hours? It was the perfect fit for an architect who loves to hear, "What if…?"

Rockwell's optimism is not magical thinking. It's an infectious enthusiasm that sweeps anyone in his path into seeing the project as grand, inspiring, and doable.

And it's no accident that this sort of electric collaboration is similar to what happens in successful theater productions. For Rockwell, Broadway is a source of energy and influence, a playground where creativity can be unleashed in real time. Like a theater director who guides actors to find new interpretation in their lines, Rockwell works with clients, colleagues, and craftspeople to find original and unpredictable interpretations of places that make people feel joyous.

This book is organized to pull back the curtain on Rockwell's process. Each project begins with his own words, the tale of where ideas came from and how they were realized. Of course, he starts with those "what if" questions, then reveals the thinking that fuels the answers.

Along the way, Rockwell's spirited magnetism has attracted many collaborations, and we invited a few co-conspirators to contribute thoughts on these long-standing connections. Included here are essays by Jack O'Brien, the great director who bonded with Rockwell as they worked on the hit musical *Hairspray*, and a conversation with Liz Diller, of Diller Scofidio + Renfro, who has "cooked up" projects with Rockwell for more than a decade. The Tony Award–winning playwright John Guare, looking at the layouts for this book, was inspired to write a ten-minute play based on an unspecified Rockwell interior.

These colleagues, as well as the clients and friends who are part of the architect's universe, have come to anticipate sparks of creative energy when Rockwell walks into a room. And they always know what will follow: "What if we…?"

Mash-up

Asking "What if...?" leads to unexpected combinations. We seek forms and materials that conventionally don't go together to create new hybrids—mash-ups that would not otherwise have been imagined.

Jaleo by José Andrés

Las Vegas, Nevada

What if you mix tapas + foosball + Dalí + taxidermy + fire + Don Quixote?

A restaurant can tell a story, one that embraces the identity of the chef, the nature of the cuisine, and also the context of the restaurant itself. At Jaleo, chef José Andrés can tell you a story about anything. If you give him a potato, he'll go deep into a narrative about this dusty, ugly tuber!

For the design of the restaurant we wanted to empower the chef. So we gave him elements like vintage library card-catalogue drawers filled with inspiration from Spain: dirt from Rioja, potatoes from Álava, an octopus in porcelain, and even a real octopus in one of the drawers. We created a stage for José. So when he's cooking and says, "Let me tell you about this turnip," he'll go pull a turnip out of the drawer. It creates a show, and José is a showman.

José brings a lot of energy to Spanish food culture, and we responded with a mix of playful elements in the environment: foosball tables and an eccentric array of commissioned artworks by contemporary Spanish architects, furniture makers, and artists. These pieces are like installation art that you experience as you move through the room. Even the façade feels welcoming, with Spanish calligraphy cut into doorsthat protrude into the public circulation of the hotel, like two open hands welcoming guests.

The centerpiece of the experience is the paella bar, a dramatic open-fire, 360-degree station. The dish arrives at your table in enormous flat paella pots, about three feet across. Just serving this meal is part of the show. Restaurants can create powerful and lasting memories, similar to the experience of live theater.

Preceding spread
Patterns, shapes, typography, and foosball are combined in Jaleo's theatrical interior.

Top
The restaurant celebrates Spanish cuisine, craft, and emerging artists.

Above
Flames leap dramatically under the grill of the purpose-built paella kitchen.

Right, top
Chef José Andrés helped choose the custom artworks, including a faux taxidermied bull.

Right
Card-catalogue cabinetry contains whimsical Spanish objects.

Chef José Andrés's Jaleo reimagines authentic Spanish traditions with a twist. It's an experience of unexpected fusions in food, design, and art. In the 7,500-square-foot restaurant, located in The Cosmopolitan of Las Vegas, Rockwell Group and Rockwell Group Europe riffed on Andrés's lively theme with an environment where guests can eat and play foosball surrounded by sculptures from Spanish designers, including Guillem Ferran, Brosmind Studio, Vibia, and Vinçon.

The restaurant's metal façade is punched with Spanish culinary terms. Created by Barcelona-based graphics studio Toormix, the typographic collage is one of many textural and experiential layers of the design. Two large wooden bars serving sangria, sherry, and tapas flank the restaurant's entrance. Underfoot, terrazzo inlaid with occasional bronze sea creatures, olives, and napkins is a play on the tapas bar tradition of throwing refuse on the floor. The Spanish mantilla, a hand-embroidered shawl, inspired curtains and laser-cut wallpaper in the main dining area. Chairs and tableware are also from Spain, and Spanish designers including Juli Capella and Mikel Urmeneta provided creative direction for colors, patterns, and other accessories throughout the space.

A separate restaurant within a restaurant, é by josé andrés, offers another homage to Spain's heritage with a private dining experience inspired by Surrealist artists like painter Salvador Dalí and filmmaker Luis Buñuel. Guests also gain appreciation for Spain's contemporary artists in a separate library-themed private dining room, where the ten-seat table is surrounded by a carefully curated selection of present-day work.

Preceding spread
A private dining room inspired by Spanish literature features wallpaper printed with books.

Above
The intimate é by josé andrés offers an eight-seat private-dining experience.

Right
Plates in the shape of plaster hands provide a surrealistic touch.

W Paris Opéra

Paris, France

Where would Marie Antoinette sleep in 21st-century Paris?

For this project, set in Paris in an elegant 1870s Haussmann-era building, the question was: How do we combine the youthful energy of a W hotel with the history and glamour of the Opéra across the street? The hotel is a wedge-shaped building that creates an opportunity for a dynamic element to flow through it. We inserted The Spark—a sinuous, black-lacquered wall embedded with a lighting system that flickers and gets more animated as night falls, an echo of the glittering evening façade of the Opéra. This central element is visible through the historic fabric of the hotel's façade and transforms many of the traditional interior details. Moldings appear solid along the perimeter wall, but as they move closer to the shimmering lights of The Spark, they appear to fragment, melt, and disappear. Taking creative risk is essential when you're trying to combine dissimilar things, and that incredible energy lies in the final mash-up—banging one thing up against another.

Preceding spread
Contemporary French artists bring a modern-day twist to the building's historic interior.

Left, top
Classic ornamentation and furniture contrast with a high-tech display wall.

Left
The curve of the bar echoes the light and energy of The Spark.

Art at W Paris Opéra

Artist Shoboshobo's *The French Kiss* in the W Lounge

Marcel van der Vlugt's modern portraits of historical French icons

Artist Ludo's signature graffiti is found in the staircase.

Emily Forgot's illustrated characters add an element of surprise to the rooms.

Zevs uses invisible ink in his trademark "liquidation" technique.

As classical moldings in an 1870s Parisian mansion begin to give way to contemporary elements, they become more noticeable; this is part of the design introduced by Rockwell Group Europe to make W Paris Opéra more than the sum of its historic and modern parts. Louis XV–style chairs upholstered in neon-hued Spanish textiles and Parisian pop art in baroque frames become part of a conversation that continues with the city's famed Palais Garnier opera house across the street. This architectural context is given a digital-age foil with The Spark, a backlit, steel-and-Plexiglas sculpture that weaves in and out of public spaces and private rooms. The perforated element ties together the hotel restaurant and lounge, DJ booths, martini bars, and each guest room, with programmable tempos and colors that change with the season, time of day, or event. The Spark also transforms nearly every element around it, bleeding into the chevron pattern on a black terrazzo floor and giving a molten appearance to a bar counter. At W Paris Opéra, the twenty-first century teases Beaux-Arts architecture at many surprising turns, whether inside or out.

Preceding spread
In the W Lounge, The Spark's vibrancy appears to break apart the classical moldings.

Above
A playful circular bed is designed for socializing.

Right
Ornate Louis XV–style chairs are paired with modern upholstery and artwork by Emily Forgot.

Aloft Hotels

Worldwide

What if a boutique hotel took a drive down Route 66?

Eight years after we created the first W hotel in New York, Starwood asked us to prototype a new kind of hotel, a little sister to the high-end W chain. Our thinking started with the romance of Route 66 roadside motels. How could we re-create that ethos in a modern, updated experience? We engineered out the crummy bar and buffet, and made those spaces one big energy center. We added a long bar, a fireplace, and a living room—unexpected luxuries that have real impact in such an efficient environment.

A full-scale prototype was built in a warehouse in Queens and tested extensively before eventual rollout. We kept the exterior porte-cochère of the early models and transformed it into an expressive element, with a linear graphic swooping up in an aerodynamic gesture. Inside, we used bold graphics to develop a blur of movement and traffic. In terms of aesthetics, we wanted to create a destination that nodded to midcentury modern design but also embraced an unpretentious, almost rec-room ambience—a mash-up of elegance and play.

Above
Aloft's identity evokes the vocabulary of the roadside motel.

Right
In the lobby, the centralized welcome desk creates a focal point.

Aloft Hotels channel classic American motel architecture into a modern, more upscale lodging experience. The concept, which has been realized in more than 110 cities worldwide, does away with the traditional full restaurant and instead provides travelers with a multiuse social environment, day and night.

At the center of the design is a concept called re:mix, a 24-hour living room where guests can check themselves in, have coffee, take a lunch break, or catch up on work during the day. In the evening, the space transforms into a lively bar-lounge that encourages travelers to spend time outside their rooms. A self-service kitchen area called re:fuel features a day-to-night bar called w xyz.

Materials and spatial configurations play to the rec-room atmosphere in public areas. Polished concrete floors and exposed plywood walls create a backdrop for more surprising and luxurious elements, such as a pool with a fireplace.

Guest rooms are designed with similar flexibility. Nine-foot ceilings and oversized windows create a loftlike space in which custom furnishings, including a wall-mounted desk and a chaise that doubles as suitcase storage, help maximize space. Wood headboards double as wall partitions between the living and bath areas. Artwork installed above each headboard is customized in every city, from Brooklyn to Bangkok.

Preceding spread
Oversized images and graphic patterns are developed for each hotel location.

Above
The light fixtures and furnishings were custom designed.

Above
The room is efficient:
A veneered headboard also
acts as a closet and divider.

Following spread
Living room spaces are
generous in scale and designed
to encourage interaction with
fellow travelers.

NeueHouse

New York, New York

What if the office became a place to live, create, play, research, entertain, connect, dine, incubate, film, broadcast, mentor, muse, learn, party, invent?

The client for NeueHouse came to us with a big idea: There's a sea change happening in the world of work that calls for a new take on the way an office environment is built. The challenge of completely rethinking the workspace touches the core of what we think about with all our projects: How do you create a space that sparks spontaneity? The project raised questions about how people collaborate, how the creative process happens, and how this is ultimately all closely tied to hospitality.

NeueHouse was one of those great opportunities where the client brought us in before they'd picked a space; it meant we could craft the concept and then find a location that would support the vision. We started with the idea that we could learn from looking at the way New York City flows, the way public space is used, and the way accidental encounters lead to connections. And then we found a perfect building with the right scale to allow for some of the same behaviors we saw outside in the city.

We wanted a living, breathing, changing organism that would be different in the morning, afternoon, and evening, and would accommodate the way people want to create together in an office. When designing a collaborative workspace, you can't predict every possible use. You have to leave a lot of the questions open-ended enough to be answered during the process. We knew we needed flexibility. I think we're really studying the intersection of daily life, theater, and architecture.

Preceding spread
A combination of fixed and movable furniture accommodates small gatherings and larger events.

Top
A custom-designed cart is used to deliver locally sourced, artisanal fare to members all day long.

Above
The Canteen also serves as a space for informal socializing and working.

Right, top
A living-room atmosphere was designed for work and meetings.

Right
Members can opt to collaborate in a library-inspired space.

The corner offices and rigid hierarchies of yesterday's workplace have broken down. Today, individuals and small startups are creating new business models that require an architectural response. Tech entrepreneurs Joshua Abram and Alan Murray founded NeueHouse after considering how best to attract new recruits to their own businesses —meeting in hotel lobbies and coffee shops just wasn't working. The NeueHouse model will be replicated in several locations around the world.

Typically, a 35,000-square-foot, five-floor office building in New York would be divided into a set of discrete functions: cubicles, conference rooms, corner offices. But NeueHouse's headquarters, at the edge of Gramercy Park, is designed to facilitate collaboration among teams of entrepreneurs and between companies and people who might

otherwise never meet. The space was created from a century-old light-manufacturing building and the former home of the Tepper Galleries auction house, and the plan incorporates elements that are more characteristic of a boutique hotel, with the feel of a private club.

On the main floor, a large enclosure houses meeting rooms, offices, and the Canteen, and culminates, at one end, in an area called The Steps—bleacher-style seating for work and casual meetings during the day as well as lectures and presentations at night. These areas also provide spaces for collaboration and client meetings, relaxation and dining, and impromptu clusters of front-stoop chats. At the lower level, a state-of-the-art screening room, radio broadcast booth, quiet library, and conference room that transforms into a dining room are springboards for connection.

Flexible seating and furniture is used in all the spaces, with movable industrial steel-and-glass partitions redefining studios as a member's company grows and shrinks. Attention to detail makes the workplaces productive and people-friendly. Whiteboard-clad studio doors and warm lighting inform day-to-day life in the space. Each area was conceived with not only a function but also an experience in mind. As evening falls, lights automatically dim, a subtle sign to members that NeueHouse isn't just for nine-to-five work; it is a place where new ideas can happen at any moment.

Above
The Steps offer prime seating for presentations.

Right
Custom movable steel-and-glass partitions allow offices to shrink and grow.

Materials

We tell stories by engaging the senses. The quality of surfaces, the tactility of fabrics, and the mood established by color and pattern are our language of materials.

Travelle at The Langham

Chicago, Illinois

How can you bring a human touch to a corporate icon?

Travelle at The Langham

Travelle, the signature restaurant in Chicago's iconic IBM Building, designed by Ludwig Mies van der Rohe, is situated in the ultimate tree house: Perched on the second floor, it features stunning views of Lake Michigan and Bertrand Goldberg's Marina City towers. We were asked to create a restaurant in this 1972 landmark that would be not just an amenity to the hotel above, but also a magnet for people who want to come and relax in a glamorous, modern environment. We immersed ourselves in imagery from the late 1960s, a time when icons of corporate culture were being built all over the country, and when the computer age was born.

The restaurant is broken up by a pair of bronze screens, which form a wall that actually moves. The wall looks absolutely permanent, yet the fact that the two screens can glide and slide closed heightens the sense of a floating, flexible space. The screens, whose design was inspired by the shapes and patterns of computer hardware, lead to a bar that is darker and moodier, thanks in part to the bronze pendant lights, which create warmth. The lounge, the slinkiest of the spaces, has lower furniture and a long feature wall with one side made of Macassar ebony and the other of polished chrome with a digital pattern. The chrome of the wall seems to shift as you pass it, teasing you with flickering reflections of the lake outside and the people inside.

Preceding spread
In the lounge, a 30-foot wall features a video installation by Yorgo Alexopolous.

Above
Chicago's Millennium Park is featured in a collage by Chris Dorland.

Right
Inside the entry, a bronze screen frames a green-onyx-and-wood check-in desk.

Ludwig Mies van der Rohe's IBM Building (now known as 330 North Wabash) is one of Chicago's architectural icons, and the youngest structure in the city to receive landmark status. The 52-story corporate modernist tower soars over the Chicago River; its façade of anodized aluminum and bronze-tinted glass is an enduring example of Mies's pioneering approach to curtain-wall design.

With a history of investing in historic properties, The Langham wanted to infuse its 13-floor, 316-room hotel with a Miesian spirit of innovation while introducing its brand of luxury hospitality to Chicago.

Travelle, a second-story restaurant and bar overlooking the Chicago River, brings these two goals together with a design that invites guests to use the space by day and evening. Travelle's

restaurant, bar, and lounge form an L shape thatflows from a glass-enclosed kitchen to an open 300-bottle wine room and chef's table. The space culminates in four separate bars arranged in a pin-wheel pattern, and in lounge seating around the windowed perimeter.

Inspired by the history of the site and by Mies's use of elemental materials and clean geometries, a pair of 1,100-pound solid bronze sliding screens creates a visual marker. The work of early German digital art pioneers, including Georg Nees and Frieder Nake, provided a jumping-off point for the sculptural wall in the lounge adjacent to the bar. Fabricated with the aid of modern digital modeling software, its 874 bent-plate units create a transformative pattern that yields a range of appearances, depending on the time of day and the viewer's position in the space. The

30-foot-long-by-18-inch thick wall includes digital art that changes, transforming the space from day to evening. Rockwell Group collaborated with The Langham Chicago and the Art Production Fund to develop a collection of work by established and emerging Chicago artists, and these pieces are displayed throughout the restaurant.

Left, top
A pivoting divider made of vertical glass tubes swings open to create a private dining area.

Left
Custom-designed tables with solid cerused oak tops reinforce a midcentury-modern feel.

Above
The high-gloss ebony surface of the bar reflects views of Bertrand Goldberg's Marina City towers.

Shinola

New York, New York

What if "Made in Detroit" could teach us new lessons in craftsmanship?

Shinola is a company built to follow a mission. For three years they've been developing products based on the intersection of American-made values and technologies acquired from around the world. Take, for example, their watches. The founder of Shinola is a master of the watchmaking business. He felt there was a hunger in the market for American craftsmanship, so he brought over Swiss watchmakers to help train a new generation of craftspeople and founded a manufacturing facility and apprenticeship school in Detroit.

Shinola took a retail space in Tribeca, a Manhattan neighborhood historically known for manufacturing. One of the things we wanted to do, spatially, was create a place that worked throughout the day, but then could be converted for evening use. We wanted a space where once you're inside, it's not a hard-sell environment. It's a place you want to come into and touch the products and experience the witty surprises Shinola has to offer.

Left
A vintage bronze world wall map references America's industrial past.

The Runwell is a watch with an American-made movement built with Swiss parts.

Swiss experts were brought to Detroit to train craftspeople in the art of watchmaking.

The Shinola factory helps to revitalize midtown Detroit.

Horween Leather in Chicago, an industry leader since 1905, employs experienced craftspeople and hands-on production techniques.

Shinola

In the fall of 2011, Bedrock Manu-facturing Co. purchased the name Shinola from the defunct shoe-polish company and established a new watch factory in Detroit's Argonaut Building, formerly the General Motors Research Labora-tory. The company's mission is to revitalize manufacturing in Detroit by producing high-quality hand-made goods that will spark new interest in American craftsmanship.

After opening one retail location in midtown Detroit, Shinola chose the formerly industrial neighbor-hood of Tribeca for its Manhattan flagship store. The space includes a 2,000-square-foot ground-floor retail showroom, café, and newsstand. A brass spiral staircase beneath an atelier-like skylight leads to a second-floor catwalk with steel railings and a 1,000-square-foot office and storage area.

Bikes, watches, small leather goods, journals, and materials throughout the store reference 1930s industrial culture. A poured-con-crete floor, vaulted plaster ceiling, and whitewashed and sandblasted brick walls are complemented by warm wood display tables and brass details like naval-grade junc-tion boxes for overhead lighting and library lamps by Chapman.

In addition to showcasing the prowess of Detroit's manufac-turing renaissance, the Manhattan retail space presents the work of local craftspeople: Pennsylvania-based Walter's Custom Cabinetry created oak display tables, and the chairs were made by Brooklyn-based Uhuru.

A fluid relationship between the store's retail area and its workshop is meant to foster conver-sations about the role of American manufacturing in today's consumer culture. Millwork that displays products during the day can be transformed at night into bleacher-style seating for lectures, fashion shows, or other special events, keeping the conversation going after normal business hours.

Above
Recent bicycle models hover above the custom display cases.

Right
A spiral staircase gives dimensionality to the shop.

Canyon Ranch

Miami Beach, Florida

What if nature told you what to do?

The original Canyon Ranch is in Tucson, Arizona, and the magic there is clearly about the backdrop—a beautiful, sculptural, sometimes harsh landscape. But Miami is an urban condition, much more vertical. Here, we felt one of the design cues should be the embrace of materials, and that touch and smell were critical factors. Our strategy was to orient guests toward the view and the ocean and bring a connection to the natural elements indoors.

People are often in some form of transition when they are at Canyon Ranch—trying new treatments and regimes, evaluating change. We wanted to demystify the experience. That led to the creation of what we think of as the "host wall," an installation made of mangrove branches and agate that cuts through the three levels of the public space. We were experimenting with the idea of a natural element that creates landmarks and can serve as a quiet guidepost.

Rockwell Group collaborated with WSG Development Company and Arquitectonica to expand upon the Canyon Ranch Spa concept with Canyon Ranch Miami Beach. The spa and hotel development immerses residents and guests in a soothing setting designed to nurture mind, body, and spirit. It includes restaurants, health and fitness facilities, and a 70,000-square-foot spa. The center of the six-acre oceanfront complex is the restored Carillon Hotel, a 1950s Miami Modern landmark joined by two new condominium buildings.

Lighting inflects natural materials to create the impression of changing textures and surfaces throughout the day. In the lobby,

columns are clad in backlit coral, an element that repeats in the resort's main restaurant, Canyon Ranch Grill, where backlit columns are formed from a wormwood veneer developed by Rockwell Group.

Weightlessness and floating are also themes. An installation of smooth stones is suspended on cables alongside the spa staircase, just as piled rocks form trail signs for hikers along a mountain path. At the spa entry, a screen mounted with orchids forms a backdrop for the reception desk. The lobby's sculpture continues through the fourth floor and hangs opposite a climbing wall, where guests can refresh mind and spirit with a view of Miami's coastline.

Preceding spread
A two-story climbing wall frames views of ocean and sky, and Banyan branches intermingle with sliced geodes in the main dining area.

Left, top
The 70,000-square-foot spa offers an oasis of water therapies.

Left
Suspended flowers welcome visitors at the spa entrance.

Above
A handmade bronze sculptural screen wall connects the yoga studio to the beach.

Nobu Fifty Seven

New York, New York

What if an architect could be as experimental as a chef?

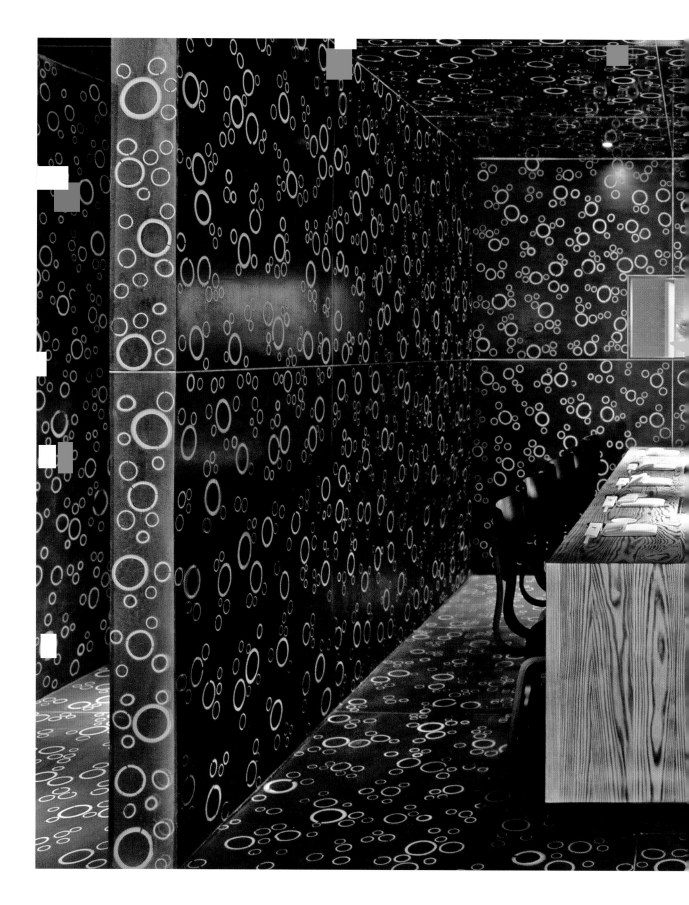

Chef Nobu Matsuhisa has been an inspiration to me since the first Tribeca restaurant we worked on together in 1994. I met him at a charity where we both contributed: I designed the event and he was a guest chef. He was already quite a star and I loved his rock shrimp! I knew I wanted to work on his first New York restaurant.

The more I learned about Nobu—his early years growing up in the Japanese countryside and his first experience as a chef in South America, where he experimented with different elements like Peruvian chili paste and ideas taken from everyday street food—the more I was drawn into the power of his cuisine as a spark for ideas. My first design impulse was to use materials in a way that explored specifics about his background and his craft. We talked about creating four gentle arches in a plan like a Japanese garden, with each one made out of a different material. The combination of rigorous, rational Eastern simplicity and Western comfort became the cornerstone of Nobu style.

Preceding spread
Bamboo has been sliced, polished, and embedded in cast terrazzo—an invention that took two years to perfect.

Left
Thousands of abalone shells make up the chandelier hanging above the bar.

Right, top
A heavy-hewn bar top appears to float above a glowing onyx base.

Right
Woven abaca screens frame the upstairs banquettes.

Rockwell Group's first collaboration with Chef Nobu Matsuhisa on a restaurant in Tribeca over 20 years ago led to a reinterpretation of the traditional Japanese restaurant. In the 1994 project, riverbed stones, woven birch branches, and scorched wood became the building blocks of the story. The vocabulary has evolved since then, and can be seen in Rockwell Group's designs of two additional Nobu locations in New York—Nobu Next Door and Nobu Fifty Seven—as well as 14 other Nobu restaurants across the globe, from Waikiki to Dubai. Nobu has grown from a restaurant into a full-fledged brand.

Fifteen years after the first project in Tribeca, riverbed stones set in a wall have become ubiquitous in Asian fusion food environments. For the design of Nobu's 57th-Street location in New York, Rockwell Group started new research, and over two years developed a fresh way to tell Nobu's story. Cast terrazzo embedded with polished bamboo, light fixtures made of abalone shells and sea urchins, and a curvilinear wall of abaca fiber echo the natural materials and craft traditions of his native Japan. Three-dimensional computer modeling allowed designers to envision the fluid forms of these hand-woven screens, which have continued their metamorphosis in other Nobu restaurants around the world.

Above
Thousands of sea urchin tentacles form the ceiling panel in the upstairs dining room.

Right
Terrazzo patterned with ripples resembles an ocean floor.

Nobu Hotel

Las Vegas, Nevada

What if a restaurant became a hotel?

After installing Nobu restaurants in hotels all over the world, the idea of creating our own hotel was something the Nobu team jumped on. An opportunity came up at Caesars Palace, which was a fascinating context for us exactly because it has so many limitations. Mostly we were constrained by the tower itself; there wasn't much we could do to change the room modules, for example. So we had to be very precise. We had to go in there with the rigor of Asian simplicity. It was like trimming a bonsai tree.

We knew that Nobu Hotel should feel like an oasis. Our tower is open on all four sides. It's in the center of a casino, so you see other restaurants and people circulating, as you would expect in a place designed for gambling. Caesars Palace is the epitome of flashy, glitzy Las Vegas, so we countered that with an almost spartan entrance and a jewellike check-in desk, handcrafted wood walls, and very simple rooms, which pair Asian minimalism with Western comfort. Las Vegas is a perfect foil that only heightens the effect of Nobu Hotel's serenity.

Left
Custom gold-leaf wallpaper with a cherry-blossom print manufactured by de Gournay floats above the bed.

Above
The bathrooms have teak fittings complemented by Japanese Umi stone tile.

Almost 20 years after opening the first Nobu restaurant in New York, the same group of collaborators—chef Nobu Matsuhisa, actor Robert De Niro, restaurateur Meir Teper, and Rockwell Group—created the first Nobu Hotel, which opened in Las Vegas in 2013. The project provided an opportunity to expand the Nobu culinary experience to create a fully immersive environment. Like the restaurants, the hotel is a defined landscape.

Located in the Centurion Tower at Caesars Palace, the hotel's entrance signals a change in tone by offering minimal furnishings and simple materials that add texture without complexity. Within the hotel's 181 rooms and suites, wood, rice paper, and stone blend with Western accompaniments, and although Nobu's medium is different, visitors see his influence in Japanese prints, photography, and expressionist, graffiti-like forms selected by the chef. Guests have private access to the largest Nobu restaurant in the world, with 325 seats, teppanyaki tables, a sushi bar, and screens that wrap the dining room, creating a distinctly Japanese experience that is both a part of and apart from the city around it.

Above
In the hotel's restaurant, semi-private dining "pods" are revealed by an upholstered Japanese fishing basket.

Right
Earth tones and natural textures evoke a sense of tranquility in the penthouse suites.

Nobu Global

New York

Next Door

Las Vegas

Dallas

Fifty Seven

San Diego

Hong Kong

Waikiki

Bahamas

Melbourne

Dubai

Mexico City

Nobu Hotel Riyadh

Nobu Hotel Manila

Budapest

Beijing

Nobu Hotel Las Vegas

Los Angeles

Doha

Moscow

Nobu Hotel Chicago

Adour Alain Ducasse

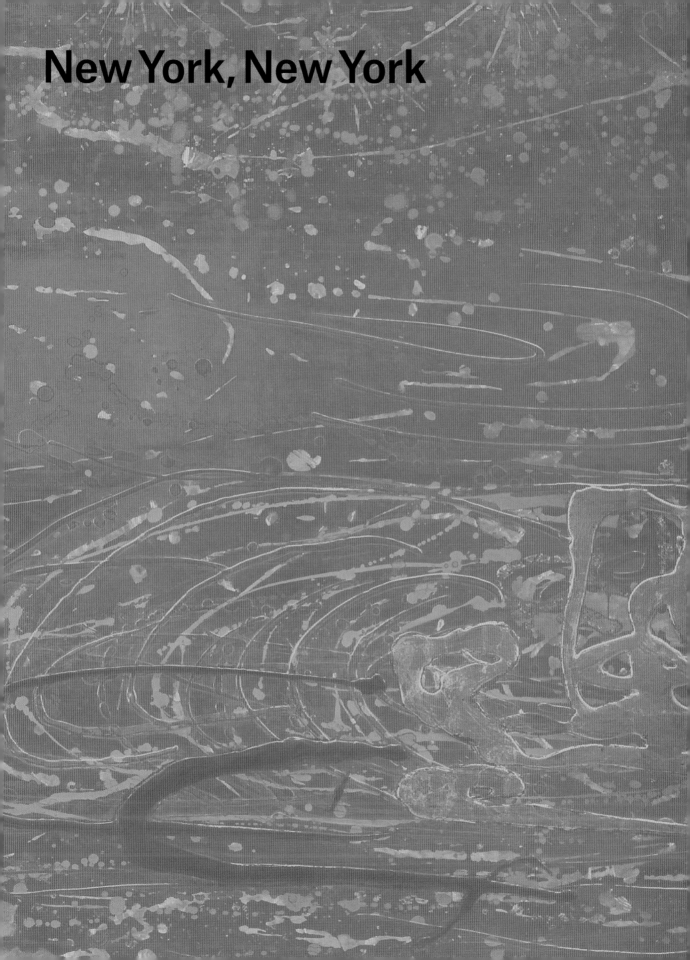

New York, New York

What if you could step inside a crystal goblet?

Adour Alain Ducasse

We wanted to create a restaurant for Chef Alain Ducasse that felt modern and luxurious, that explored wine and its pairings with food. We thought it would be interesting to turn it inside out, to make what is normally invisible in a restaurant—the decanting and wine service—visible by placing a sommelier's station at each corner of the main dining room. Next we translated a theatrical scrim into glass and wrapped it around the entire main room. We used three layers of glass; the one closest to the public is made of slumped glass, which has a handcrafted feel. We stenciled a pattern onto this layer in a translucent hue very close to the color of Bordeaux, which we found by holding the wine up to light and observing the color that was reflected through it. By applying aluminum leaf with a platinum wash on the wall, adding this glass scrim, and then lighting the space between the surfaces, we were able to create a relationship between the newer and older rooms. The space between those two layers also gave us the perfect place to create a temperature-controlled environment for almost 3,000 bottles of wine.

Preceding spread
A love of wine drives the
Adour experience.

Above
The color palette of the
room features Merlot red
and Champagne gold.

Right
Traditional moldings are visible
behind a modern glass scrim.

An environment to immerse newcomers and oenophiles alike in the exploration of wine, the 88-seat Adour Alain Ducasse at the landmarked St. Regis New York combines interactive technology with a less formal atmosphere that references Chef Ducasse's upbringing near France's Adour River.

The restaurant's intimate four-seat wine bar, crafted by sculptor Brad Oldham, has a bronze base and features an interactive sommelier. The technology, developed by Rockwell Group in collaboration with Potion, allows guests to peruse the restaurant's seasonal selection of approximately 500 wines. By moving a hand across the bar, users activate a motion-sensitive projection system hidden in the ceiling, revealing a display of topics related to the wine's characteristics and origins.

Four decanting stations in the dining room allow guests to watch their sommelier prepare wine to be served. The stations are designed with a curved wooden top and an uplighted wine bucket at one end. All of the restaurant's bottles are out in the open. The dining room, inspired by a library reading room, is surrounded by four temperature-controlled armoires of burled mahogany and antique bronze, which display the collection.

Old and new elements interact in inventive ways in the restaurant's interiors. The existing architecture is covered in platinum leaf and enveloped in a glass veil decorated with a laminated film interlayer of an abstract grapevine pattern by local artist Casey Maher. The back of the main dining area features three private dining rooms: the rectangular Vault Room, and the Left Bank and Right Bank, which are oval in plan and have antique-mirrored ceilings. These are connected by the rectangular River Room, featuring a five-panel mural of the Adour River by New York artist Nancy Lorenz.

Above
An interactive sommelier is accessed through a motion-sensitive projection.

Right
The private Vault Room features leather-covered personal wine vaults.

B   I don't think I'll tell you.

A   Tell me the worst thing you've ever done in your life. Make me hate you or be repelled or look at you with a dropped jaw.

B   Why?

A   It'll make all this more bearable if I hate you.

B   That's so easy. The Valley of the Kings.

A   As in Egypt?

B   I was a student. Years ago. Hitchhiking. Daring to hitchhike. Europe. The Middle East. No strife back then. A world that said, Look at me. Learn from me. Take me. Enjoy me. Egypt. December. Empty. No tourists. A hitchhiker I had met told me not to miss a recently discovered tomb in the Valley of the Kings. I went there. Asked. Got lost. Asked a man with a camel. I found it. No ticket takers. No guides. Open door. I stepped into the dark. Found the stairs. Held onto a rickety banister going way below ground level. Down, down, down. The air was stale. No, not stale. Ancient air that no one had breathed for thousands of years and now was being inhaled by me. I loved the tombs. The Egyptians had a marvelous sense of proportion. Very geometric. Very comforting.

A   The tomb. You're in a tomb.

B   Oh yes, the tomb. I walked down, down, down. I heard voices.

A single naked light bulb dangled from a beam. It lit the image of a human figure with the head of a bird painted on the wall. What was—A tour group led by a guide speaking English stood under a single light bulb. The guide deciphered the images. This tomb, this king. See his bird head. That is his Ba. We all have a Ba. Our personality. Our character. See this figure holding out his hand in welcome? That is his Ka. The life force. The part of us that is immortal. The two parts of a human—his personality, his life force separated at death. The Ba would meet the Ka on the other side of the underworld, and be reunited for eternity. I was entranced. The guide suddenly stopped. Someone is listening to this talk who has not paid to be on the tour. This person is stealing information that was purchased by you. I will not go on until that intruder leaves. The group turned and glared at me. I begged pardon and went to another part of the tomb which went lower and lower. The air was stale. Another single light bulb showed me the wall paintings. Which was the Ba? Which was the Ka? The tour appeared—the guide started explaining the paintings—see the Ba united with the Ka—I listened from behind a column. He saw me—I will not continue speaking until everyone who has not paid good money to be on this tour leaves the tomb— the group turned to me. Silence. Rage. I capitulated. I felt for the stairs and went up and up and up and up. I could hear the guide's

voice growing fainter and fainter below. Ba Ka Ba Ka. I stepped out of the black tomb into blinding Egyptian sun. I looked around the Valley of the Kings. No one was around. I saw the light switch. I clicked it off. Screams below. I slammed the door shut and went to find someone dependable like King Tut.

A   You turned off the lights and slammed the door?

B   What right did they have to exclude—What right did they— Every now and then I hear those voices from that tour pleading, Turn on the lights. Open the door. Give us air. Please—let us out! I still hear them. I wake up. Are they still down there? So many times I've felt that I'm in a tomb breathing ancient air. The opposite of this place. The lights turned off. Flights of stairs. A lack of oxygen. A locked door.

A   You did that?

B   I'd do it again. Shall we have one more course?

A   That's a famous unsolved mystery in Luxor.

B   What are you saying? Keep your voice down.

A   The dead tourists. December? All those years ago? A deserted part of the Valley of the Kings? A recently discovered tomb. Twenty eight people found dead—suffocated.

B   No!

A   It's been one of the most famous unsolved mysteries in the annals of tourism.

B   What are you saying?

A   That's you? All these years later to solve a crime that's crossed over into legend. The twenty-eight bodies at the top of the stairs died pounding against the locked door. No one heard. December. No tourists. No air. The sun baking down. The heat. Who was the monster who had locked them in? Oh god—you? Horror. You had committed a crime. That is the worst thing I ever—I believe the Egyptian government offered a reward for information leading to—that should come in handy covering the bill for this meal.

B   You're joking.

A   I wish. Do you have constant anxiety gnawing at you?

B   I was a student. It doesn't count.

A   This crime would explain that constant anxious gnawing at your innards. Do you have bad luck?

B   From time to—Yes. I do.

A   Your legendary bad luck is payment for this crime. The naked eye sees. I finally see you.

B   Don't look at me.

A   Everyone in this restaurant is staring at you. They see you.

They slide their chairs away from this table. I thought I was the center of their attention. But it's you. Everyone sees your crime.

B   I was young.

A   Go back to Egypt. Confess. You have no choice.

B   Isn't there a statute of limitations?

A   Not in Egypt.

B   Oh god—

A   I'm kidding you.

B   What are you saying?

A   Keep your voice down. Smile. My pathetic attempt to inject levity into this—what is this meal? Lunch? Dinner? Supper? We came here. We weren't hungry. We needed time. Of course you didn't kill them. At least not that I ever heard. If you had, the Egyptians would've quashed a story like that. The Egyptian government can't afford to have dead tourists on their hands. They depend on their tourists. As a restaurant depends on its clientele. Don't get any ideas. Don't think you can get up and turn off the lights and slam the door and leave. That won't work here.

B   I didn't kill twenty-eight people?

A   None that I ever heard of. Bravo, very good story.

B   It's not a story. It's the truth of me.

A   It makes me not like you.

B   I'd lock that door again if I had the chance.

A   And yet here in this ambience you're a paragon. Restaurant angel. Desert devil.

B   Please.

A   Tell me more about the Ba and the Ka.

B   I've told you all I know. It's ancient times. This room. This texture. This light. This ambience.

A   When I die, will you be my Ka?

B   It's time we—

A   When you die, will I be your Ka?

B   It's time we—

A   Time we—

B   Time we—

A   Just a moment more. Don't leave. This room.

They reach their hands across the table.

Storytelling

All environments tell a story. Quiet visual cues can evoke a Roman trattoria; croissant pavers can conjure Paris for a movie set. Details create new worlds.

Ames Hotel

Boston, Massachusetts

The story of the Ames Hotel in Boston starts with a gorgeous property. It's a white limestone building from 1889, a highly detailed, monochromatic, Romanesque Revival structure. We wanted to find a way to link the design to the city of Boston and, more specifically, to the Ames family, a wealthy and influential Boston Brahmin clan who were leaders in the agricultural tools business. Throughout the hotel we embraced the idea of sculptural objects and commissioned art work for our installation.

For the restaurant, The Woodward, we wanted to link the two-story space to the hotel, but we wanted it also to have its own identity so it didn't feel like an add-on amenity. We brought in a local artist, Sally Moore, and Silver Hill Arts, a group we work with here in New York, and we all went on a search for vintage agricultural tools and objects to create large-scale, Joseph Cornell–inspired environments. Almost a hundred sculptural creations made from agricultural tools sit in Plexiglas boxes throughout the restaurant and line the staircase, making the journey from the ground floor to the second floor a passage through time.

Preceding spread
The original ceiling has been adorned with a Mylar chandelier.

Left, top
Illuminated cases display familiar and curious tools, a reference to the Ames family business.

Left
A ceramic wall installation by Draga Susanj takes cues from the vaulted ceiling in the lobby.

A Cabinet of Curiosities

A walnut display table houses a collection of eighteenth-century pipes.

Sally Moore's whimsical sculptures give new life to historical objects.

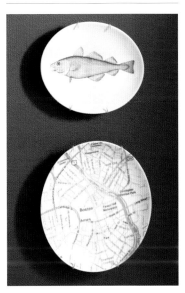

Morgans Hotel Group collaborated with Harry Allen Design on custom plates to be hung in each guest room.

The 13-story Ames Building, designed by Shepley Rutan & Coolidge in the Richardsonian Romanesque style and completed in 1889, was Boston's first skyscraper. Redesigned as a luxury hotel for Morgans Hotel Group, the property tells the story of the one-time corporate headquarters of the Ames family's agricultural tool company, using modern-day details to create a narrative the hotel described as "Benjamin Franklin meets a supermodel."

In the lobby, the building's original marble mosaic-tile vaulted ceiling and a marble-and-brass staircase are the backdrop for a chandelier designed by Rolf Knudsen of London-based Studio Roso. The chandelier, with its hundreds of reflective Mylar discs suspended on wires, provides a contemporary counterpoint to the opaque mosaic pieces. Behind the reception desk is an orange-and-white site-specific ceramic wall installation by Draga Susanj, made of hand-sculpted pieces in an abstract form inspired by the building's exterior fire escape and vaulted ceiling.

Like the lobby, the two-story hotel restaurant is also an amalgamation of eras, fittingly named The Woodward after an eighteenth-century tavern once owned by almanac author Nathaniel Ames. The restaurant's interior walls are painted white, bringing a monochromatic lightness to exposed steel columns, brick walls, and ceramic floor tiles that are original to the building. The main feature of the space is a cabinet of curiosities composed of eight Victorian-inspired cases placed throughout the dining area and containing 120 handmade and historical objects.

Representations of nineteenth-century industry continue in the hotel's corridors. Here, guests are greeted by a Pepper's ghost, a theatrical device that creates the illusion of a crystal chandelier floating behind a mirrored wall. A contrast of history and innovation, the effect provides a dramatic point of entry into lofty, light-filled guest rooms decorated with touches of Federal style.

Above
Dramatic windows are featured in the one-bedroom apartment suite.

Right
An ensuite bathroom is a high-contrast study in geometry.

Maialino

New York, New York

What would a Roman trattoria look like in Gramercy Park?

Maialino

Every project has its own DNA. It's built by engaging a client up front to develop a unique narrative of what their project should express. For Maialino, restaurateur Danny Meyer presented a number of ideas. One was that he wanted this to be experienced as a local restaurant—it's on Gramercy Park, one of the few private parks in the city, which gives it a European flavor. Danny also wanted Maialino to be a destination for all three meals of the day, which is interesting because New Yorkers don't tend to eat breakfast where they eat lunch or dinner.

We thought about ways the room could feel connected to its location, and at the same time transform subtly over the course of the day. Danny was excited about the idea of creating a true Roman trattoria. We had a breakthrough when we started to talk about the rituals of trattorias and suggested that we could build the space around those rituals, physicalizing them in key places. We talked about the kind of relationship that exists between customer and waiter, and the sense of generosity that was very much a part of both the local trattoria model and who Danny is as a person. We created an open food prep area in the middle of the space, and you walk through it to reach the dining room in back, which banquettes subdivide into two smaller areas. That put food and service, hospitality and generosity at the center of the restaurant, and everything else is oriented around it. It's the focus on hospitality that makes it feel like a neighborhood place. And that's what a trattoria is; it's a small community.

Preceding spread
Desserts and breads are displayed in cases made from reclaimed wood.

Left
The *salumi* station brings life to the center of the restaurant.

Above
Brightly colored stone-tile floors frame seating for breakfast, lunch, or dinner.

Left
Informal blackboards
display daily specials above
the elegantly simple bar.

Left, bottom
Booths with woven-leather
upholstery are carefully placed
along a back wall.

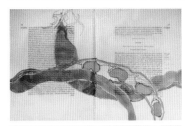

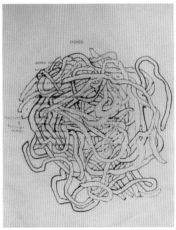

Works on paper by Robert Kushner, who also
created the murals in Danny Meyer's Gramercy
Tavern, are hung informally around the
restaurant. They feature images of produce
included on Maialino's Roman menu, painted
on pages from Italian books.

Danny Meyer's Maialino (Italian for "little pig") transports guests from the busy streets outside to a neighborhood restaurant situated inside Ian Schrager's Gramercy Park Hotel. With windows overlooking Gramercy Park, the restaurant's three-part layout flows from a café and bar at the front to an open kitchen at its center and to a dining room at the back. The spatial orientation puts the message of food and hospitality at the forefront: Wine bottles and dessert service are out in the open, and a *salumi* station, long walnut bar, and large communal table that seats 22 establish an easy-going atmosphere. Visible from the street, the café draws guests inside during the day and into the evening, when it transforms into a wine bar.

To capture a sense that interior elements had been collected over a long period of time, materials, colors, and textures express Italian inspiration mixed with authentic New York industrial design. Rustic Amish white oak ceiling beams were reclaimed from a demolished log cabin in New Jersey and wainscoting is made of reclaimed white oak from Pennsylvania. Rather than create replicas of trattoria light fixtures, Rockwell Group commissioned hand-hammered fixtures from New York–based O'Lampia to contrast with the restaurant's traditional elements.

The Walt Disney
Family Museum

San Francisco, California

What if a biography was told in three dimensions?

So much of Walt Disney's life is documented through films and interviews that we realized his own voice could tell the story at The Walt Disney Family Museum. Spatially, we began with an account of his development as an artist. Like most creative individuals, his work started out in a linear fashion and then became multi-dimensional. We used the more intimate spaces of the building to illustrate his early roots and then tracked his development as a creative visionary. From beginning to end, the journey has a lot of impact because it goes from a very narrow single point to a three-dimensional matrix.

Disney had many losses in his life, and they often fueled his most creative work. To meld his story to the architecture of the building, we delve into a three-dimensional map of the ten years of his most incredible output. A ramp pathway connects his activities—from TV, to film, to parks, to feature films, to the technology he invented. For me, one of the most compelling aspects of the exhibition is how it highlights technology in service of storytelling—a lesson for the technology-drenched world we live in.

We knew the visitor would already be familiar with some of the material on display—and familiarity can lead to contempt! So we wanted to make it new again. For example, there's a whole room that reveals the technical advances in *Snow White and the Seven Dwarfs.* One image that's amazing to me is the wall of paint jars full of the studio's proprietary colors. Looking at the hundreds of pigments and how they were used in the development of voice, character, movement, and color lets us get inside what we think we know about Disney.

Preceding spread
A 164-foot spiral ramp solved the complex 3-D puzzle of how to lead visitors through the museum without using stairs.

Above, top
Views of San Francisco Bay complement an installation of the many documentaries Walt produced.

Above
Personal stories, like Walt's marriage to Lilly, are intimately presented via densely hung photographs and recorded voice narration.

Right
On the mezzanine, 20 vintage televisions show animations and archival footage.

Walt wanted the deer in *Bambi* to be very believable; two real-life fawns were brought into the studio to be studied.

Samples of paint jars and color keys from the studio's vast palette of proprietary colors

Merchandising brought characters like Dopey to life for fans in a new way.

The Walt Disney Family Museum is a three-dimensional documentary about the life of one of the world's most creative storytellers. Located in an 1898 barracks building on the Presidio's Main Post in San Francisco, the museum's 18,300 square feet of exhibit space presented an opportunity to tell Walt Disney's own story using the tools that were most important to his career: art, music, and technology. The project was a chance to rethink traditional exhibition presentation; at the same time, collaborations with individuals who knew him best—including his daughter, Diane Disney Miller; her husband and former company CEO, Ron Miller; and 25-year Disney Imagineer Bruce Gordon—brought an important layer of anecdotal history to the museum.

Exhibits contain mixed-media presentations—projectors, monitors, and sound installations—but avoid creating a distraction with visible technology. In the second-floor gallery, six monitors play some of the 56 animations Disney created in the first few years of his career, including 400 drawings for *Steamboat Willie*, which amount to 17 seconds of animation. Interactive tables with touch-sensitive bronze instruments like a ratchet, lip pop, boxing bell, and cat scream demonstrate how sound effects were applied to cartoons. On the fourth floor, visitors can crank through the frames of an animated scene using a Moviola, a small machine once used for playing back reel outside of a screening room.

The museum pulls back the curtain on one man's genius. It's a reminder that before there was Mickey, there was a man named Walt Disney.

Left
Hundreds of drawings show the making of *Steamboat Willie*.

Above
Historical film footage contextualizes the thousands of objects on display.

Yotel

New York, New York

What if the bellhop was a robot?

Yotel was an opportunity not only to create a new hotel on the edge of Times Square, but also to be involved in MiMA, the larger, mixed-use complex that houses it, and for which we also designed the public spaces.

Yotel is based on the notion of air travel. The rooms are quite small and therefore called for an intense calculation of every inch. They needed to be efficient but they also have an embedded sense of luxury, more like a first-class lounge or airline seat. In the rooms the bed is automated and mechanized so that it can become a sofa; the story of the room can change at the push of a button. The pleasure of transforming it not only makes the room more comfortable, but engages the guest in an experience that is linked to the magic of high-end air travel.

In each room a dimensional wall has specific spots for everything: places for your luggage, your clothes, your keys, and even the remote control. That kind of compact, built-in character relates to my fascination with futuristic Italian design from the 1970s, such as Joe Colombo's inhabitable Total Furnishing Unit. Working within the constraints of a very compact space challenged us, but constraints are, of course, the essence of the very best design.

Preceding spread
At 15 feet tall, the Yobot has an expansive reach and can retrieve your luggage in 30 seconds or less.

Above
Dramatic lighting accentuates window frames and edges.

Right
A nightstand also functions as a desk.

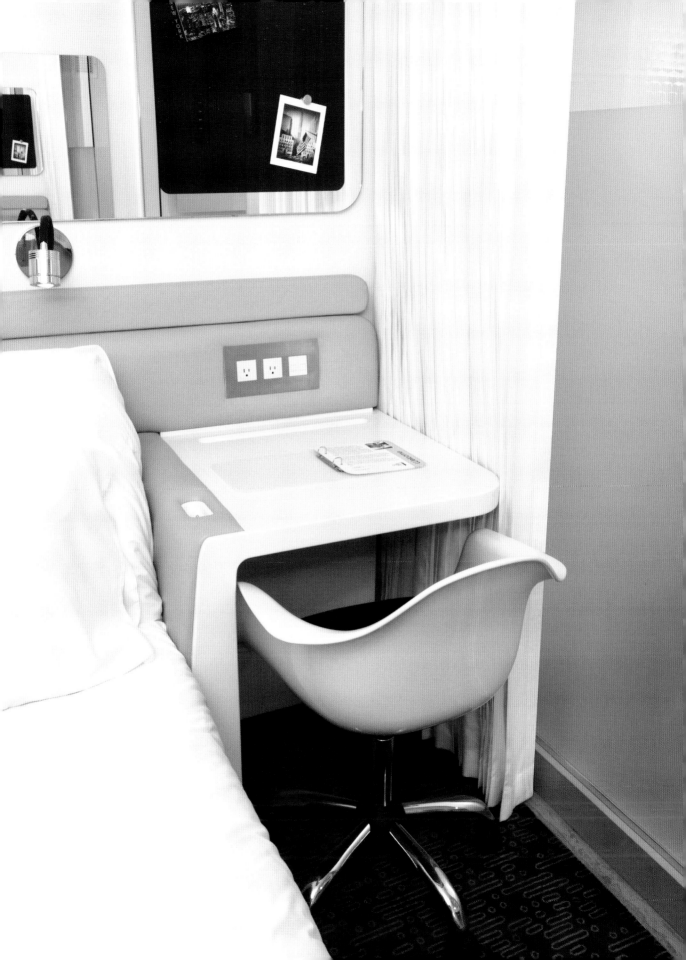

A futuristic, techy hotel set within a larger residential building embeds efficiency in first-class luxury. Part of Related Company's $800 million LEED Silver certified MiMA (Middle of Manhattan) complex, Rockwell Group's Yotel marries Japanese capsule hotels with the pleasures of top-notch airline travel. Before coming to Manhattan, Yotel properties had always been attached to airports, where international travelers could book a room for just a few hours between flights, as well as by the night.

A robotic arm—dubbed "the world's only robotic luggage concierge"—theatrically stows baggage in the lobby, and a 20,000-square-foot terrace defines the fourth-floor public area. In the restaurant, long tatami-inspired tables retract into the floor to make room for dancing. Guest rooms, each about 10 by 17 feet, also feature convertible furniture with beds that transform into space-saving sofas.

The MiMA complex occupies a whole city block totaling over 1.2 million square feet, including the Frank Gehry–designed Signature Theater, restaurants, retail, and 663 rental and 151 condominium units.

Left
The hotel's public areas include private cabins for meetings or parties, cozy sitting areas, and a view of a vast outdoor patio.

Above
The restaurant mixes sumo wrestling imagery and a dance floor.

TAO Downtown

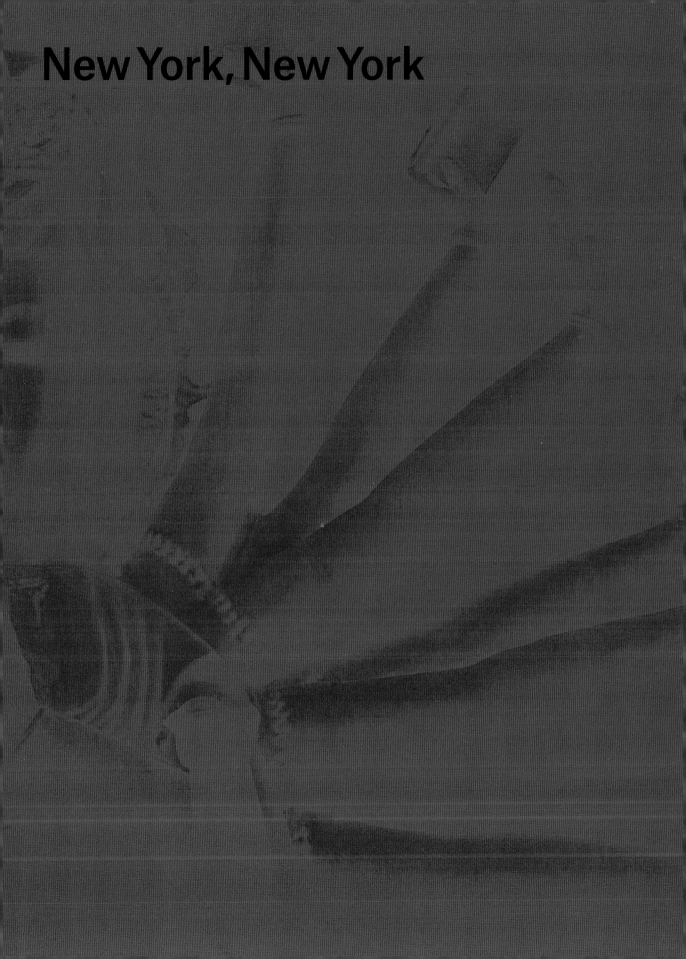

New York, New York

What if you could dine on the steps of a deity's temple?

With TAO Downtown, we were invited to tackle dining as theater—but I felt like it was a slightly lazy description, in that *theatrical* tends to be a limiting term that conjures up images of something bedazzled and fabulous. There's nothing wrong with that, but this was an opportunity to push the thinking further, and to delve into ideas about choreography that we had been exploring for many years.

Logistically, we had to negotiate a 16-foot change in elevation from the entry level to the main restaurant floor. Because we were combining two existing spaces within the Maritime Hotel, we were able to place an entrance mid-block on Ninth Avenue, then create a processional walk that brought guests around to enter the room as they might enter any great theatrical presentation.

I began to think about the ways in which stairs play into an audience's arrival at a performance venue. My lifelong fascination with stairs is in some respects due to their ubiquity in Manhattan (the high cost of ground-floor real estate means you contend with stairs every day). From an experiential point of view, you might descend a stair into a performance space or climb up, as you do at Radio City Music Hall. So, as we played with the stair here, the question I was intrigued by was: What if the whole restaurant embraced the staircase?

Bringing the Deity to Life

The Rockwell Group LAB used 3-D projection mapping technology to animate and continuously transform the 20-foot-tall Quan Yin statue.

A shadowy flock of birds

Moss seems to grow almost imperceptibly.

Robes flutter in a digital wind.

A cavernous, subterranean space in Chelsea's Maritime Hotel, TAO Downtown is an Asian-inspired Gotham speakeasy. As guests descend into the 22,000-square-foot space from street level, a host, stationed in front of a dragon-scale-patterned screen, leads them down a grottolike path. Along this corridor, Chinese calligraphy murals atop weathered brick introduce an exotic ambience and materiality that continues throughout the bar, restaurant, and lounge.

While this entry into the Ink Bar, TAO's mezzanine-level lounge, is intimate, the restaurant's grand 1,300-square-foot staircase is designed to create a spectacle. It leads guests into the main dining room, producing a see-and-be-seen experience for those arriving and for anyone lounging on the Chinese daybed–inspired sofas placed on its spacious landings.

TAO's impressive scale is echoed in its architectural elements: Over-sized bent-wire lanterns hang from the ceiling, and an 18-foot-tall Quan Yin stands atop a koi pond at the far end of the restaurant. A symbol of compassion, the statue seems to change continuously throughout the course of an evening. To create this illusion of movement, Rockwell Group's LAB designed five animations using 3-D projection mapping technology to move across the multi-armed statue.

The collision of ancient craft and advanced technology, and of Eastern with Western cultures, is underscored in Rockwell Group's collaboration with Hush, a UK-based artist who combines street art and traditional techniques to create mixed-media work. Installed on the exposed brick back wall of the Ink Bar, Hush's 19-foot-long, 6-foot-high mural depicts dragon figures

in a collage of paint, poster paper, vellum, bonding glue, and shellac. Rockwell Group installed a series of 6-foot-tall hammered-wire-and-glass panels over the mural to give it a pixelated effect. In the adjacent lounge, Hush's second mural, of graffiti geishas, is painted on floor-to-ceiling exposed brick walls and continues along the staircase to the cellar level. The progression suggests a cave filled with ancient drawings, adding to the transformative dining experience found in the heart of New York City.

Above
A larger-than-life statue watches over a waiting area near the upstairs lounge.

Right
The artist Hush painted his graffiti geishas directly on the wall behind the bar.

Team America: World Police

Hollywood, California

What if the actors are two feet tall?

Team America: World Police is probably the most surreal project we've ever been invited to work on. I'm a huge fan of Matt Stone and Trey Parker, and they had an idea to do a movie in the style of *The Thunderbirds*, the classic British marionette TV show. *Team America* was meant to be satirical and present a particularly American point of view of the world— it's a travelogue, seen through the eyes of puppet heroes or antiheroes.

One of the things that became interesting to us was to play with the scale of the sets. The marionettes are only about two feet tall, and we wanted to hint at this by creating a series of "Where's Waldo"– inspired environments. Embedded within each set are partially hidden elements that represent the movie's Americanized view: The pavers in Paris are made out of cast croissants; the only vehicles in Times Square are yellow taxis; and Kim Jong-il's village is made out of Chinese takeout containers.

The city of Paris was the first set we designed, and in some ways it was the most challenging because it's so big and so recognizable. We thought it would be interesting to take all of the best-known monuments from Paris and put them in one scene—so the Eiffel Tower, the Louvre, the Arc de Triomphe all exist in one little plaza, atop croissant pavers and amid little French poodle topiaries. It's a combination of what real Paris looks like and what people going to EPCOT might think Paris looks like. Throughout, we tried to create a world that had its own bizarre logic—a reductive American view of the world.

Preceding spread
Kim Jong-il is rendered as a piano-playing puppet.

Above
An early model shows Paris covered in logos.

Right
Two-foot-tall puppets ride past croissant-shaped pavers.

Following spread
The sets were designed using extremely forced perspective— the buildings behind the Eiffel Tower are 10 feet away and less than 12 inches tall.

Team America's headquarters are built into the face of Mount Rushmore.

Overloaded with American icons and graphics, Team America's vehicles are garaged outside HQ.

Terrorists around the world are tracked from this hipster setting.

Team America's watering hole has a waterfall feature wall.

Team Base riffs on the Wrightian house in Hitchcock's thriller *North by Northwest*.

High design continues with a nod to Liberace's favorite clear piano.

In this terrorist hangout, the bar is made out of toxic waste cans.

The bronze statue between the staircases in this scene is an actual person.

Traditional Korean details are mixed with Vegas-like ostentatiousness in a palace described as "dictator chic."

Just like the real Times Square, this set is a dizzying brandscape filled only with yellow taxis.

Lisa's bedroom features Marc Newson's iconic Lockheed Lounge.

In Gary Johnson's New York dressing room, miniature bricks cover the walls and playbills tile the floor.

Croissants appear as pavers in Paris.

Chess pieces are stand-ins for bollards.

Playbills tile the dressing-room floor.

Torpedos hang from lanterns in Kim Jong-il's palace.

A Philippe Starck juicer takes the role of a floor lamp in Lisa's bedroom.

The craftsman's hand is revealed in Rockwell Group's design for the film *Team America: World Police* by Matt Stone and Trey Parker, the duo who created *South Park*. Rockwell's design plays with scale, creating an unexpected visual language through simplified views of cities. The far-flung backdrops for the cast of marionettes include Paris, Cairo, New York, Kim Jong-il's palace, and the team's headquarters, situated within Mount Rushmore. The design riffs humorously on cultural clichés when, for example, Chinese take-out containers become vernacular housing and shredded dollar bills become Hollywood palm trees. Occasionally, the designers sprinkle in elements that reveal the marionettes are only two feet tall.

Left, top
Inside the headquarters are a little Noguchi coffee table and a Nobu-inspired undulating wall.

Left
Matt Stone and Trey Parker on set

Above
David Rockwell in Kim Jong-il's miniature palace

Stagecraft

Stagecraft drives the emotional story arc of theater. Highly technical and precise, it is designed to make a lasting impact with just a brief encounter.

Set Design

What if the set became a character?

Kinky Boots

Kinky Boots is the unlikely story of Charlie, a third-generation kid in Northampton, England, who inherits his father's shoe factory, which he doesn't want. Then he meets Lola, a drag queen in London with similar father issues. Charlie and Lola decide to reinvent the factory to cater to the burgeoning global drag-queen market. Every piece of the set is used in more than one way: conveyor belts become the stage for a big production number; shoe racks move back and forth to create a kind of magical transition. The craftsmanship of the sets was our link to Charlie's work in the factory.

Director: Jerry Mitchell
Writer: Harvey Fierstein
Composer/Lyricist: Cyndi Lauper

Bank of America Theatre, Chicago
Al Hirschfeld Theatre, New York

Left
Billy Porter, at center, plays the character Lola/Simon.

Right, from top
Gritty details onstage; the factory's conveyer belt doubles as a moving platform for dance; the sets magically transform from the factory floor to a glamorous runway show in Milan.

Following spread
Dramatic shifts in lighting help define the change in scene.

Michael Pitkin
David Poole
Ron Walton
Steve Wolin
Lee Wright
Michael Erikson
Emilio de Olivares
Ray Wheeler
Roger Malendra
Nino
Bruce Mailman
Phil Mantelker
Royal Marks
Leonard Matlovich
Court Miller
Ed Moore
Stewart Gerber
Brian Becker
John Robinson
Jay Merritt
Mark Machnik
Jon Boswell
Christopher Clanda
Perry Ellis
Howard Rachlin
Tom Morano
George Morton
Tim Corns
Phillip Gilmore
Thomas McDowell
Bill Klowman
Keith Keen
Cascoe Bruton
Jamil Garland
Cary Scott Lowenstein
Richard V. Irizary
Lance Hardy
Arnold Bankston
Stuart Mabray
Tom Gardner
T. Scott Cunningham
Larry Burke
James Roy Jackson
Robert Lasser
Cliff Duer
Thomas Showestull
Bill Shuttleworth
Michael Reisenberg
Michael Goldstein
Stephen Langston
Tom Gardner
Paul Walker
Bob Davis
William D'Acutis
Larry Kert
David McFarlane
Michael Bennett
Jim Boatwright
Bobby Borland
Michael Brody
Roscoe Browne
Alan Buchbaum
Jody Callahan
Lynne Carter
Lee Goodman
Herb Gower
Tobin Greene
Richard Greene
Peter Grimes
Michael Grumley
Sam Haddad
Ric Horton
David Summers
Michael Taylor
Carl Thomas
Bruce Thompson
Jacques Tiffeau
Juan Miguel Torres
Abel Perez
Hibiscus
Antonio Lopez
Gregorio Ramirez
Jacques Belanger
Gilles Bourghard
Jean Guy Dion
Fernando Delgado
Mundo Meza
Coenraad Stegeman
Mario Ghelardi
Marco Ravalcaba
J. Victor Lopez
Ignacio Zouro
Elizabeth Prophet
Marco Lodovico
Louie Galicia
Dayna Jo Lynn
Mario Marozi Sebastian
Louis Padilla
Peter Glo
Grady Mulli
Gary Barker
Rick Rockwell
Clay Holland
Neal Hanlon
Steve Jacob
Frederick Goodhow
Stevan Popovic
Pat Bonfiglio
Esther
Ramon Flores
One Sweet Eld
Woman
Lords
Carol L.
Olga L.
Shirley Z.
Sandy Colon
Diego Lopez
Donna
Nina
Tanya
Violet
Carlos Mampeviz
Raul Casares
Wanda
Weny
Susan Jackson
Niklaus Debret
Harvey Wang
Rainer Wolf
Rene Ramo
Paul Dietens
Debbie Miller
Fritz Schmacher
Crystal Laspe

The Normal Heart

The Normal Heart is a play about the AIDS crisis, written in 1985, before the epidemic had a name. Together with the directors George C. Wolfe and Joel Grey, we conceived of the set as a memorial to the heroes finding their voices and fighting the disease. The main set walls display a collage of writing about AIDS from 1985. We also project names directly onto the surface of the set; these multiply throughout the play as more and more people are lost to the epidemic.

Directors: George C. Wolfe, Joel Grey
Writer: Larry Kramer

John Golden Theatre, New York

Left
The names of people lost to the epidemic are projected and the lists grow as the play progresses.

Right, from top
Projections animate static walls onstage; projections by Batwin + Robin Productions spill offstage into the theater itself; 3-D letterforms appear when lit at an angle; the offices of the *New York Times* are indicated using an oversized clipping from the paper.

Lucky Guy

Lucky Guy is Nora Ephron's final play; it is about the tabloid columnist Mike McAlary. When director George C. Wolfe invited me on board, I set about researching how 1980s and '90s newsrooms looked. We couldn't be bogged down with heavy transitions, so we pared the sets down to a couple of elements, like a grid-hung ceiling to create a sense of compression and to give us a surface to project onto. Minimal, weightless set pieces allow the actors to quickly manipulate fragments of scenery and bits of furniture to suggest the variety of locations required by the story.

Director: George C. Wolfe
Writer: Nora Ephron

Broadhurst Theatre, New York

Above, top
This researched depiction of a 1980s newsroom includes unapologetic smoking.

Above
Simple, movable furnishings and careful lighting allow two scenes to exist at once onstage.

Right
Tom Hanks starred as the Pulitzer Prize–winning reporter Mike McAlary.

A Free Man of Color

A Free Man of Color is a vast, surreal collage written by John Guare and directed by George C. Wolfe. Set in New Orleans in 1801, around the time of the Louisiana Purchase, it weaves the story of a wealthy man, Jacques Cornier, with those of many historical figures, using a tremendous 33-member cast. Our storytelling begins simply, but very quickly there is a series of dramatic surprises that take place on the thrust— virtually in the audience's faces. This interplay continues, shifting from fore-ground to background, from moments overloaded with visual information to moments of bold abstraction.

Director: George C. Wolfe
Writer: John Guare

Lincoln Center Theater, New York

Left
A high level of detail in the mural and bed is contrasted with playfulness in the draping of the fabric.

Right
Working models were used to help visualize the abstract, graphic sets and shifts of scale between scenes.

Legally Blonde

Legally Blonde tells the story of Elle Woods, a Southern California girl who is unexpectedly accepted to Harvard Law School. Working with choreographer and director Jerry Mitchell, our challenge was to create 22 place locations and also allow seamless transitions between them. Elle's optimistic sorority world is largely pink, while the authoritative world of Harvard is all burnished dark wood. Through the use of scrims and lighting, the scene can change from Harvard to Elle's world in a millisecond.

Director: Jerry Mitchell
Writer: Heather Hach
Composers: Nell Benjamin, Laurence O'Keefe

Golden Gate Theatre, San Francisco
Palace Theatre, New York

Below
A large graphic scrim gives a sense of depth to the stage.

Right
Windows and pieces of a gate are all that is needed to represent the campus—the audience fills in the rest.

Following spread
Elle's world is depicted using a combination of highly realistic bedroom elements and abstract lighting.

CQ/CX

CQ/CX (the title is journalistic shorthand for a checked/corrected fact) is a project we did with director David Leveaux. Gabe McKinley's script tells the well-publicized story of reporter Jayson Blair, a rising star at the *New York Times* who, in 2003, was found to be plagiarizing and fabricating parts of his stories. To capture the feeling of the newsroom, we explored mostly flat imagery on four different planes—a rear wall and a series of louvered screens. The overhead ceiling grid is in a sharp, forced perspective, which puts the audience right at the center of the action.

Director: David Leveaux
Writer: Gabe McKinley

Peter Norton Space, New York

Left
Lighting corresponds to particular states of emotion.

Below
This transformable set uses ceiling panels and office-grade venetian blinds as surfaces for projection.

PLAYBILL

CIRCLE IN THE SQUARE

PLAYBILL

NEIL SIMON THEATRE

hairspray

PLAYBILL

VARIETY ARTS THEATRE

OMNIUM GATHERUM

PLAYBILL

PALACE THEATRE

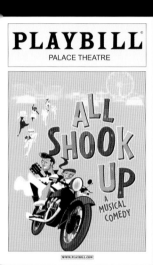

ALL SHOOK UP
A MUSICAL COMEDY

PLAYBILL

IMPERIAL THEATRE

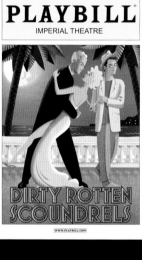

DIRTY ROTTEN SCOUNDRELS

PLAYBILL

PALACE THEATRE

LEGALLY BLONDE
The Musical

PLAYBILL

DUKE THEATRE

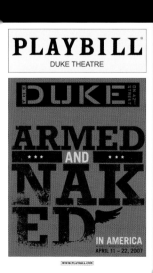

THE DUKE ON 42ND STREET

ARMED AND NAKED

IN AMERICA
APRIL 11 – 22, 2007

PLAYBILL

SECOND STAGE THEATRE

NEW YORK PREMIERE
LET ME DOWN EASY
CONCEIVED, WRITTEN & PERFORMED BY
ANNA DEAVERE SMITH

PLAYBILL

VIVIAN BEAUMONT THEATRE

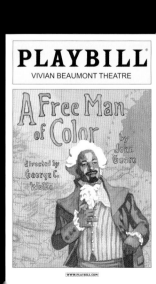

A Free Man of Color
by John Guare
directed by George C. Wolfe

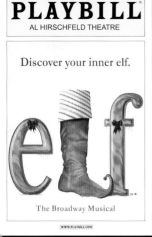

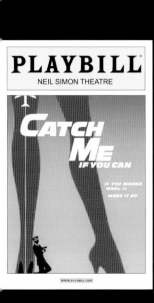

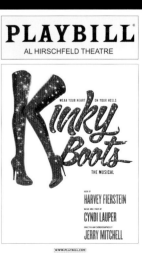

What If... Indeed!

Reflections on a creative partnership

Jack O'Brien

I met David Rockwell over a dozen years ago for breakfast at a café on Union Square. Jerry Mitchell, my choreographer, told me I should talk to him about a new musical we were doing—*Hairspray*. We all laughed. We parried and thrust a bit, but mostly we asked, "What if...?" Those words came up again and again. I used them, Jerry used them, but David defined them! "What if we did this?" "What if we could use that?"

Here's how David does a "what if": Sitting in the apartment of Marc Shaiman and Scott Wittman, the composer/lyricists of *Hairspray*, we glanced up at a gigantic image of Ken, Barbie's boyfriend. It was composed of bits of illuminated plastic in Lite-Brite, the children's toy. Jerry called our attention to it, but David seized on the moment, the concept, the riot of color. And that became the underlying metaphor for a Tony-winning Broadway musical.

A flurry of ideas began to tumble out of him. There were strong architectural requirements implicit throughout the show. For example, we needed a lower-middle-class living room that could accommodate an ironing board, a television set, and a musical dance number at the same time. Then we needed a sixties record shop in a ghetto neighborhood, not to mention a store that sells jokes and novelties. If a Broadway show ever called out for the mentality of an architect, *Hairspray* shouted for one.

The fascinating problem, and the one we had to tackle first, of course, was that the score had at its heart the famous "wall of sound" principle so prevalent in the music of that period. Each number was augmented by an entire chorus of back-up voices. Where would they stand? How would we build them into the show?

Early in the process, I wondered if there shouldn't be more of a studio feeling to the production, a place where the singers could watch the show, then pop down and join in during their numbers. Instead, David devised towers far upstage— a kind of abstract jungle-gym of shapes that was used in all the large ensemble numbers. For the iconic opening song, "Good Morning, Baltimore," the singers on the towers were silhouetted behind a scrim to set up the pumped-up look and sound of early sixties Baltimore.

David knew that he would need a set equal to the larger-than-life characters of the musical. He would have to supply a context that mirrored the irresistible pulse of the score, and he offered witty solutions that originated in an architect's universe, yet served as a visual trampoline for our irrepressible characters to bound upon. He also realized he would need to begin the evening by keeping all color at bay until he could finally explode his Lite-Brite vision with an energy that matched the story. Leading up to that, he found countless charming and original touches that built to the finale, like having a Motown trio step out of a two-dimensional billboard and come to life on the streets.

And eventually, faced with the dilemma of topping himself for a finale that couldn't "stop the beat," he invented an environment lifted from the futuristic obsession of the period—the Eventorium—with its rocket-shaped arches that managed to send up period architecture with perfect wit.

It was then that I knew I had found an invaluable artistic partner in someone capable of honoring the real but in love with the fantastic. So off we went to do *Dirty Rotten Scoundrels*, where David took us to the other end of the spectrum. For this musical the palette was meant to evoke the elegance and the wealth of the French Riviera, a location that would suit a sly, charming felony taking place at the center of the plot. You wanted to feel the perfume in the air. David gave us that Mediterranean feeling of a gorgeous, endless summer with beautiful light. Even the palm trees were silhouetted with jewels, because we wanted everything to have a kind of glitter to it.

For *Catch Me If You Can*, which like *Hairspray* is set in the sixties, we went from maximalism to minimalism. David had to give me places for scene work that explained what the story was about, because the musical numbers didn't necessarily do that. The key to the show became David's bandstand, with a live band on stage that recalled a lot of early television spectaculars with orchestras, and this became a constant large-scale prop.

And now we're taking on *Houdini*, a deferred dream of unimaginable challenges ahead of us. But each time we embark on a project, the ball flies back and forth between us with the invaluable "what if" that has become core to a creative partnership.

Oh, yes, David is a control freak, all right! But the miraculous thing is, you never actually feel it. What you see is what you have happily managed to accomplish together. There is no field in the performing arts as demanding of collaboration as the musical theater. It is not the single artist facing a canvas. It's an entire phalanx of egos, inspirations, instincts, minds, all individually convinced they alone have the exact right note of music, the right blocking, the right fabric, the right gel, the right to make the event perfect. However, no one survives the experience alone: one must embrace every individual contribution. And that is where David triumphs. There is contained, within his "what if," no knife, no bludgeon, no imperative. There is only the gentle opening of an undreamed door, beyond which one is invited to go.

Choreography

By defining entrances, creating pathways, and making motion part of the design, we give space a tempo and rhythm.

Hall of Fragments

Venice, Italy

What if your environment transformed with every step?

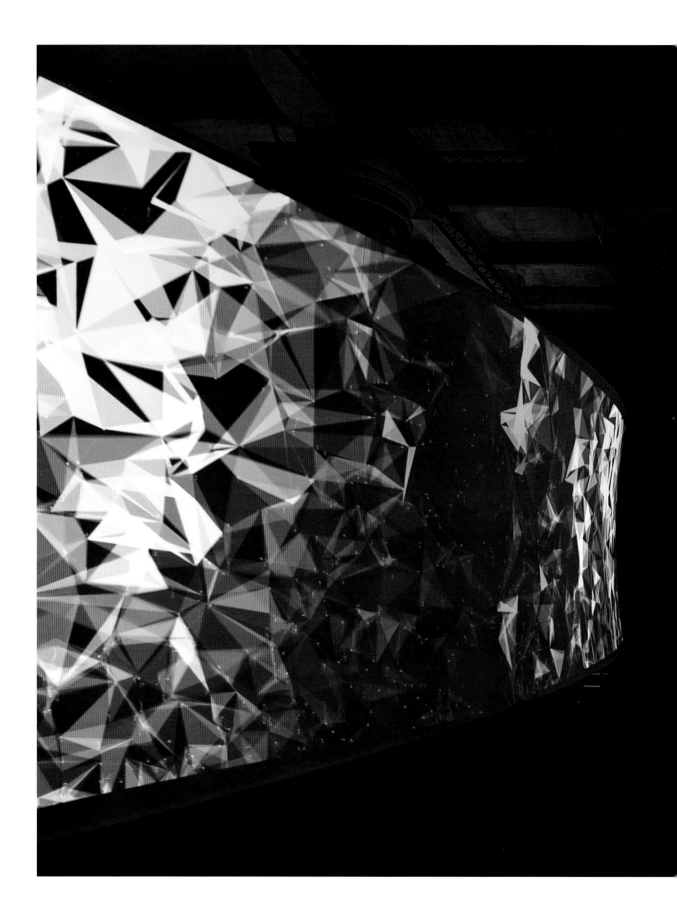

Choreography

For the 2008 Venice Architecture Biennale, we were invited to create the exhibition that visitors would see first upon entering the nearly quarter-mile linear path of rooms in the Arsenale.

Hall of Fragments was all about movement. Visitors stepped in from Venice to an environment whose motion sensors automatically summoned fragments of cinematic worlds. You could engage in different ways. Sensors activated short clips of films as you moved through, but by standing behind the concave scrims, you could see the activity of people without actually seeing them. So by being there you were both a witness and a participant in the choreography.

This was the first large-scale installation that we created with our LAB team, which became a launch pad for much of the work we're doing today, about the intersection of performance, architecture, and technology.

The 11th International Venice Architecture Biennale, held in 2008, was based on the theme Out There: Architecture Beyond Building. Rockwell Group's response to the idea was called Hall of Fragments, and was positioned as the first installation in the Biennale's main hall, the sixteenth-century Corderie dell'Arsenale. Developed by Rockwell Group's LAB and designed in collaboration with Reed Kroloff and Casey Jones, the 4,600-square-foot space brought visitors into an interactive environment built of iconic film clips, each featuring alternate architectural universes created in cinema.

Two concave screens covered with tensile fabric filled the 60-foot-long hall. Using motion-detecting infrared cameras, the hall's kaleidoscope of shapes and electronic soundscapes responded to the visitor's movement. Behind the screens, 68 monitors displayed short clips of movies featuring notable built environments. Hall of Fragments emphasizes the way in which public space can stimulate the senses and encourage people to interact when freed of brick-and-mortar restraints.

Preceding spread
The installation served as an introduction to the Biennale's main hall.

Left
15-foot-tall screens immersed visitors in an environment that constantly changed.

Fragments of Worlds:
Architecture in Film

2001: A Space Odyssey

8 1/2

A.I.

Blow-Up

Citizen Kane

Cleopatra

A Clockwork Orange

Dr. Strangelove

Edward Scissorhands

Enter the Dragon

The Fountainhead

Harry Potter and the Sorcerer's Stone

Howl's Moving Castle

The Hudsucker Proxy

The Matrix

Minority Report

Satyricon

Superman

Belvedere Hotel

Mykonos, Greece

What if light was your primary material?

We thought the play of light in the space over the course of the day could be one of the cues for our redesign of the Belvedere. Our strategy explored the transition from day to night, which allowed us to take advantage of the existing elements in a creative way. For example, why not give the pool furniture slipcovers for evening? It creates a new look and offers a different perspective on the same beautiful site. For me, the most interesting day-to-night transition happens around the turndown service in the hotel rooms, which can be either a magical moment or that horrible knock on the door to put a bad chocolate on your pillow. We thought that this change in time should correspond to a change in the room, so we developed a series of millwork wall screens that conceal votive candles. The daytime look is a very beautiful bright daylight, and then the nighttime look is about the flicker of relaxing flames.

The idea of transitions also applies to the way people move within the space. A series of curves leads guests from the top of the hillside hotel to its lower levels, creating a sense of anticipation as they move through spaces of compression and release. Inside, you move parallel to the view of the sea, and then all of a sudden the view is exposed. It's a kind of seduction that works really well with the site.

Preceding spread
In the upper lounge, metal-hammered custom lighting is inspired by the Aegean Sea.

Left, top
Warm whites and natural materials set the tone at the intimate check-in desk on the upper level.

Left
A rosewood screen frames the guest library.

Many of the rooms feature a generous bath with a luxurious freestanding tub.

Evening turndown service includes candlelight, specialty bedding, and signature drinks.

Crisp sheets and leather-wrapped headboards bring a wash of Mykonos white to the rooms.

The Greek island of Mykonos has long been a favorite spot for fashion shoots and high-style visitors. It is just as famous for its flattering sunlight as it is for the countless candles and lanterns that illuminate its streets and villas at night. The renovation and expansion of one of the island's most beloved hotels, the Belvedere, combines transformative lighting with textures and materials inspired by the Aegean Sea. Like the winding streets of the surrounding village, a meandering pathway through the hotel leads guests through spaces and experiences that change throughout the day and evening.

The three-level plan begins at the top of a hill, where guests are greeted in an understated reception area. Descending one level, visitors discover a lounge flanked by curved plaster banquettes and 3-foot-tall rosewood screens, hand carved as if by sea currents.

On the lowest level is a full-service restaurant with an outdoor dining area beneath a canopy of Bougainvillea vines and white flower-globe lights. The restaurant spills into the pool area, an arrangement that allows poolside cabanas to be refashioned into intimate dining rooms. Lighting transforms the space during the evening pool service, when custom-designed outdoor lanterns illuminate the pool and pergola area as the hotel's second restaurant and bar become a nightclub.

The guest rooms also take on a new look in the evening, when two unique turndown services cater to either sleep or entertaining, with new bedding, candlelight, and signature music and scents. Yacht-inspired rosewood furniture conceals ample space for clothing and shoes, ensuring fashionable guests can transform themselves from day to night as well.

Above
After hours, the serene poolside is reconfigured for a lively social scene.

Right
The restaurant, Matsuhisa Mykonos, features two outdoor dining areas.

JetBlue,
JFK International Airport

Queens, New York

What if passenger flow moved to the rhythm of air traffic control?

When we started working with JetBlue, I first reflected on all my terrible experiences in airports, which was a very deep portfolio! I thought about how in any airport, arrival gates are never close to baggage claim, and I wondered what dictates the layout. Then I started noticing signage, which is complex because airport layouts are complex. So much about the experience seems non-intuitive. JetBlue's challenge to us was to create a place that worked with 20 million people moving through it every year.

My early experiences as a kid walking along the streets in New York have left a lasting impression. I remember finding the rhythm of the city where movement through it no longer seemed blocked by people—I realized there was a kind of dance happening that was the key to a high-traffic experience. So, as opposed to being afraid of being in a building with thousands of other people circulating within it, that fact could be the joy of it. What if you could encourage movement that felt like the pace of the city? There could be express lanes and, for more leisurely meandering, slower lanes. And in the most New York moment of all, you could step up on a front stoop and get a look at the swirl and choreography of everyone around you.

At Grand Central Station, the clock in the Main Concourse is a point of focus to orient travelers. Balconies offer prime viewing of the scene below.

New York's Union Square is an oasis in the city; raised several steps above street level, it has the feeling of an urban stage.

Famously studied by William H. Whyte in his book *The Social Life of Small Urban Spaces*, Paley Park is an urban foyer.

The steps at the Metropolitan Museum of Art invite performance and performers.

Preceding spread
With 20 million passengers a year, Terminal 5 is one of the nation's busiest thoroughfares.

Right
Two islands were built to help filter fast-moving from slower-moving traffic.

The soaring walkways and spacious seating areas of Eero Saarinen's landmark 1962 TWA Flight Center at New York's John F. Kennedy International Airport inspired a new way of thinking about the design of JetBlue's Terminal 5. Other gateway structures that combine areas for walking and sitting—Grand Central Station and the front steps of the Metropolitan Museum of Art, for example—also offer models for shaping travelers' movement through the space. Rockwell Group looked for ways the urban experience could overlap with the travel experience to complete a scope of work that included dynamic wayfinding graphics and a clear signage system, as well as optimized use of natural corridors created by the terminal's architects, Gensler.

Viewing the airport as a microcosm of city life, and by turn as a theater for public life, Rockwell Group first enlisted Tony Award–winning choreographer and director Jerry Mitchell to collaborate on a study of airport terminal circulation patterns. The high-concept move of bringing a choreographer on board resulted in real-world solutions to common airport frustrations by giving passengers pathways for rapid motion and also areas for seating.

To encourage fluid movement, Mitchell advised finding ways to avoid having passengers walking in straight lines, so the terminal alternately encourages fast motion, slower motion, and rest. At the crossroads of three main concourses, a marketplace creates a range of experiences, from shopping to people watching. A grandstand and platform unite the marketplace with other areas of the terminal, creating a seating area from which to see departing and arriving passengers. Overhead, a swirl of steel cables suspends a digitally programmed information yoke in the air, leaving the concourse level open for foot traffic. Composed of 43 LCD screens, with a custom-built software platform created by the Rockwell Group LAB, the ring can host anything from information updates to site-specific digital art.

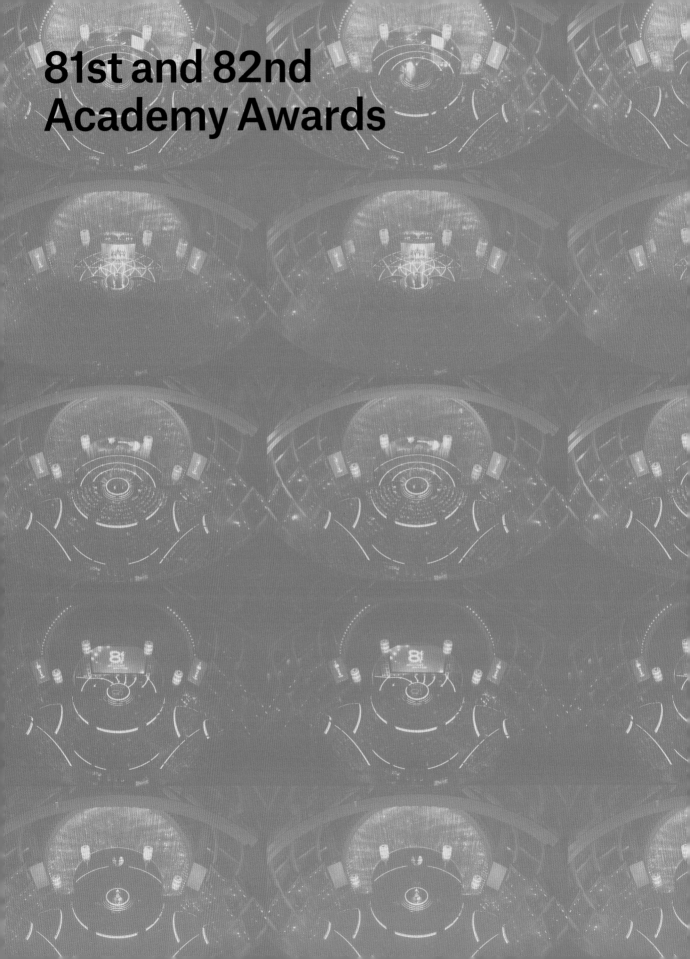

81st and 82nd Academy Awards

Hollywood, California

What if the biggest show on earth was the most intimate one?

I can tell that a project is the right fit for us when it's 50 percent terror and 50 percent thrill. Designing the Oscars was exactly that. How do you take one of the great worldwide rituals and rethink the design to change the experience? My goal, as much as possible, was to make it a live encounter for television viewers. As research, I watched 15 or 20 years of Oscars, and a theme emerged: The most memorable moments were spontaneous events, little things that weren't planned. To see an interaction, to see a kind of community, is what gives the event life. In a sense, that's a way to return to the spirit of the early Oscars, which were originally held as grand dinners at a supper club.

We started by ripping out seating and redesigning for a proscenium stage to bring the audience close. This allows viewers to see the reactions of celebrities seated in the theater. The most important thing design can contribute is a memorable sense of occasion, and the feeling that this can only happen this one night.

Left, top
Seating was moved closer to the stage, enhancing the connection between the star-studded audience and presenters.

Left
A reflective second layer of curtains was created using large metallic spheres.

Top
A sound-stage set is revealed and activated with suspended screens.

Above
Large-scale LED screens bring recent winners back to the stage.

1937: Early Academy Awards presentations, such as this one at the Biltmore Hotel, had a supper-club feeling.

1969: A catwalk brought spatial drama to the ceremonies' standardized seating arrangement.

2009: Rockwell's lighting design for the Academy Awards is inspired by Joseph Urban's use of deep blue in his design for Mozart's *Don Giovanni* in Boston. The onstage pattern that radiates from a central point recalls the Campidoglio in Rome.

David Rockwell was the first architect invited to design the set of the Academy Awards. In 2009, and again in 2010, the firm reached a new standard for the more than 80-year-old ceremony with sets that incorporated innovative theatrical production techniques.

Work began not on the stage but in the theater, where semicircular rows of chairs that wrapped the stage replaced original linear audience seating (part of Rockwell Group's 2001 design for the Kodak Theater, now the Dolby). The typical moatlike separation between performers and guests vanished—only four steps separated the audience and presenters—and the full orchestra was placed onstage in a mobile bandstand.

The sets are designed to cultivate the feeling that the ceremony's events can never be reproduced. During the 81st Academy Awards, in 2009, the evening unfolded like a Broadway show to reinforce the theme How Movies Are Made. This meant set changes couldn't happen during commercial breaks as in previous years—scenery would move in full view of the entire audience. In the 2010 program,

themed Love of Movies, dynamic sets created multiple compositions of performers and presenters, speeding transitions throughout the evening. To reinforce the lively, fast-paced transitions, the stage integrated LEDs and projected images, which along with moving sets created a constant play of light and activity. Mirrored surfaces reflected both audience and performers, while bands of faceted glass acted like vertical venetian blinds, creating the illusion of deep space on stage.

Above it all, a crystal curtain added a striking headdress-like frame to the evenings' performances, and also solved an architectural challenge by balancing the size of the proscenium arch with the arch of the stage. Made of nearly 100,000 Swarovski crystals, the piece debuted in 2009 and made its encore in ombré topaz the following year.

Left
The 60,000-pound curtain is made of Swarovski crystals hung on 2-inch centers and backlit by moving lights.

Above
Suspended cabinets contain objects inspired by the nominated films.

Elinor Bunin Munroe
Film Center

New York, New York

What if there was a world of film below Lincoln Center?

Nine or so years ago we got a phone call from the Film Society of Lincoln Center and we started a conversation about finding them an expanded home. I thought it would be a great opportunity to be involved in re-imagining this aspect of Lincoln Center, and a rare privilege to be able to work with the client while they were choosing a venue.

Lincoln Center is a nexus of high culture, which can make it feel daunting to some people. Our mission was to create a more informal and inviting gathering place within the complex. It's intended to be Lincoln Center's public living room for watching movies. One of the challenges was that in order to get enough height for the screening rooms we had to go deep enough into the space to excavate beyond the area where the mechanical plant for the whole Lincoln Center campus sits. The result is a project nestled under Lincoln Center that might be small but signifies the accessibility, spontaneity, informality, and the social interaction around cinema. The box office leaps right out onto the sidewalk, and the amphitheater is a fantastic place for public conversations.

Preceding spread
The 90-foot-long glass frontage wall, designed in collaboration with Diller Scofidio + Renfro, creates a welcoming entrance.

Left, top
The underground parking garage became three new theaters: two traditional cinemas and one amphitheater for public events.

Left
Hundreds of LED lights are embedded flush with the ground to create a sparkling carpet.

Above
The new amphitheater is a space for presentations and conversations.

As the city grows denser, New York's subterranean spaces take on increased value. In a belowground parking garage, Lincoln Center found a new home for the Elinor Bunin Munroe Film Center, a state-of-the-art multiscreen theater and cultural venue. With a 65th Street entrance, the underground space is sandwiched between the Milstein Pool above and the mechanical plant for Lincoln Center below. Sidestepping the machinery in the plant, Rockwell Group placed two screening rooms deep inside the former garage.

This spatial solution left a large gap that became an opportunity to design a public area with an amphitheater for public programs and a café for dinner before a movie. In a nod to the space's previous incarnation, a 16-foot-wide folding garage door opens the amphitheater to the lobby. The theater is one of Lincoln Center's most accessible venues, allowing visitors to purchase tickets just minutes before an event. Its entrance reflects this openness: a 90-foot-long glass façade and bright orange glass vestibule transform 65th Street into an inviting threshold.

Left
The maple wood ceiling is punctuated with acoustical slots and appears to wrap around the amphitheater.

Above
A garage door on the rear wall of the amphitheater opens the room and allows the stage to be seen by passers-by on the street.

Transformation

Transformation allows design to be light on its feet. A built environment can arrive when needed and disappear when its job is done.

Imagination Playground

Worldwide

What if you could make playgrounds portable, and kids could ask, "What if...?"

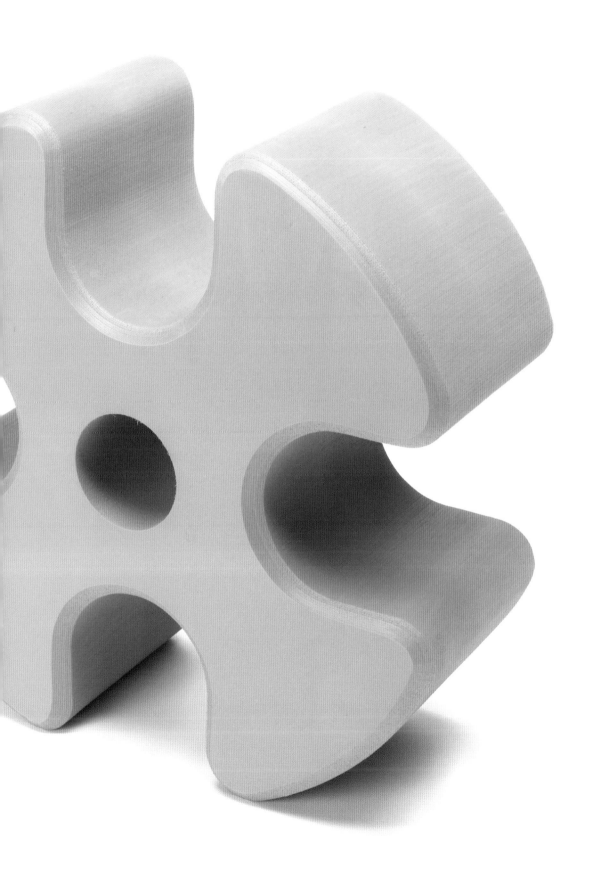

Imagination Playground

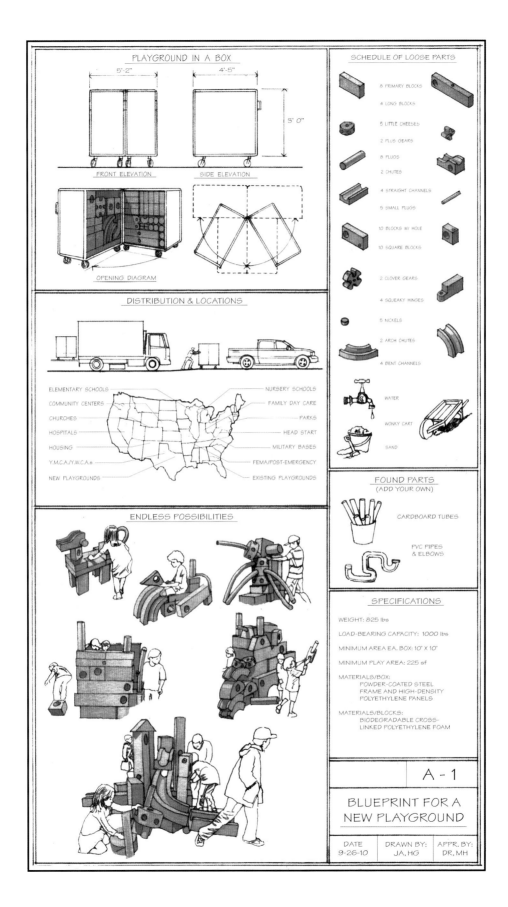

PLAYGROUND IN A BOX

FRONT ELEVATION 5'-2"

SIDE ELEVATION 4'-5" 5' 0"

OPENING DIAGRAM

DISTRIBUTION & LOCATIONS

ELEMENTARY SCHOOLS — NURSERY SCHOOLS
COMMUNITY CENTERS — FAMILY DAY CARE
CHURCHES — PARKS
HOSPITALS — HEAD START
HOUSING — MILITARY BASES
Y.M.C.A./Y.W.C.A.s — FEMA/POST-EMERGENCY
NEW PLAYGROUNDS — EXISTING PLAYGROUNDS

ENDLESS POSSIBILITIES

SCHEDULE OF LOOSE PARTS

8 PRIMARY BLOCKS
4 LONG BLOCKS
5 LITTLE CHEESES
2 PLUS GEARS
8 PLUGS
2 CHUTES
4 STRAIGHT CHANNELS
8 SMALL PLUGS
10 BLOCKS W/ HOLE
10 SQUARE BLOCKS
2 CLOVER GEARS
4 SQUEAKY HINGES
8 NICKELS
2 ARCH CHUTES
4 BENT CHANNELS
WATER
WONKY CART
SAND

FOUND PARTS
(ADD YOUR OWN)

CARDBOARD TUBES

PVC PIPES
& ELBOWS

SPECIFICATIONS

WEIGHT: 825 lbs

LOAD-BEARING CAPACITY: 1000 lbs

MINIMUM AREA EA. BOX: 10' X 10'

MINIMUM PLAY AREA: 225 sf

MATERIALS/BOX:
POWDER-COATED STEEL
FRAME AND HIGH-DENSITY
POLYETHYLENE PANELS

MATERIALS/BLOCKS:
BIODEGRADABLE CROSS-
LINKED POLYETHYLENE FOAM

A - 1

BLUEPRINT FOR A
NEW PLAYGROUND

| DATE 9-26-10 | DRAWN BY: JA, HG | APPR. BY: DR, MH |

This project emerged from watching my own kids in playgrounds, which led to a deep dive into the nature and importance of play. We looked at how and where play is most child-directed, and learned a lot from the postwar Adventure Playgrounds in Britain, where kids made things from found objects—two-by-fours, pieces of wood, buckets, doors. The kids were inventing and building their own playgrounds.

Though initially we had a specific New York site in mind, Imagination Playground became a research project about play, and about why today's playgrounds don't have a wider variety of play options. The project led us in lots of interesting directions, and over a five-year period we developed this concept.

We discovered that since the late 1960s, creative risk had been engineered out of play for many reasons, including safety and a generally more litigious world. But in thinking about play spaces for kids, we started to believe that in fact kids need fewer mandates, more open-ended play. The lesson we learned from Adventure Playgrounds is this: If you let kids do what they do best, which is create their own world, they'll find play much more engaging.

Preceding spread
Children explore Imagination Playground blocks at the Rockwell Group–designed playground at Burling Slip, New York.

Left
"Blueprint for a New Playground," an op-ed created for the *New York Times*, shows how a simple idea can result in endless possibilities for play.

Early Block Play

1820: S. L. Hill of Brooklyn mass produces ornamented alphabet and building blocks.

1837: Friedrich Froebel develops progressively complex assortments of blocks, to instill abstract thinking.

Circa 1900: Professor Patty Smith Hill invents wooden floor blocks. The larger blocks let children create environments at their own scale.

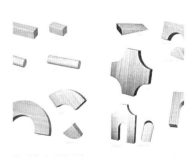

1914: Caroline Pratt invents the classic unit block set that we know today.

Imagination Playground began as an idea to create a new type of playground at the South Street Seaport in Lower Manhattan. Inspired by David Rockwell's own children, the project was an opportunity for Rockwell Group to investigate play and envision ways to reintroduce creative risk—not physical risk —into modern playground design.

The finished product, a portable collection of giant blue foam blocks, allows children to build their own play environments. Loose, lightweight parts in a range of cubes, bricks, cogs, curves, and cylinders encourage unstructured play free of the linear action that comes along with typical contemporary playgrounds—standing in line for a turn on a slide or swing, for example. The large size of the blocks also increases social interaction and collaboration as children work together to move them and construct temporary worlds.

Versatility is built into the idea. The concept was first tested in a series of "play dates" at schools and parks throughout New York. Hosted with educators and a growing coalition of individuals and nonprofits interested in redefining play, the events revealed that children not only played longer with the kit of movable parts, but also that each day they created completely new games or designs from the same set of blocks.

Today, these portable playgrounds have been deployed at schools, museums, churches, hospitals, and parks. The nontoxic blocks are designed for indoor and outdoor use and are available in boxes, carts, and bags, making them easy to transport. The design has also become part of an initiative to bring play to disadvantaged children in developing nations; to date, the UNICEF P.L.A.Y. Project has brought the power of play to more than 13,000 children in Bangladesh and Haiti.

With an estimated 1,500 Imagination Playgrounds in use globally, the face of play is changing around the world.

Preceding spread
The blocks adapt to water play in Brownsville, New York.

Above
Play, Work, Build, at the National Building Museum, was designed to exercise both muscles and minds.

Right
The blocks are just the right size to encourage collaboration and group problem-solving.

Jamie Oliver's
Food Revolution Truck

Nationwide

What if we put the teaching kitchen on wheels?

In 2010 we joined forces with Jamie Oliver, who had just been awarded the TED Prize. Jamie is on a mission to combat diet-related diseases through food education. His obsession and dream is to teach everyone, particularly kids, how to cook and eat healthy food. Not just tell them about healthy food, but engage them by letting them make it themselves. As part of his TED Prize project, we were asked to think about taking his teaching concept and putting it on wheels, making an experience that would be immersive and unforgettable.

I was immediately attracted to the idea of a mobile teaching kitchen: It has multiple states, and there is a promise of transformation and change. It allowed us to create an opportunity for kids to experience something memorable through something that is temporary. The back of the truck has an inflatable amphitheater, which is probably my favorite gesture. As it's driving around, it's a box; when it sets down, it magically opens up, creating a moment of surprise. The thrill of the circus coming to town, something that's there for only a brief amount of time, can create deeper memories than something that is always there. The truck is about being more agile, not needing to build a permanent piece. It's not there when you don't need it, and it's able to create a kind of intervention in places that may have been overlooked.

Top
An inflatable amphitheater at the rear of the truck creates a stage for events.

Above
Kitchen components can be secured with straps when the truck is in motion.

Right
The truck's sides expand to accommodate eight cooking stations and the inflatable amphitheater.

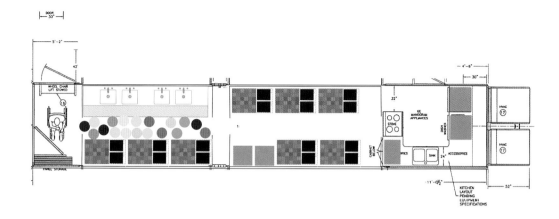

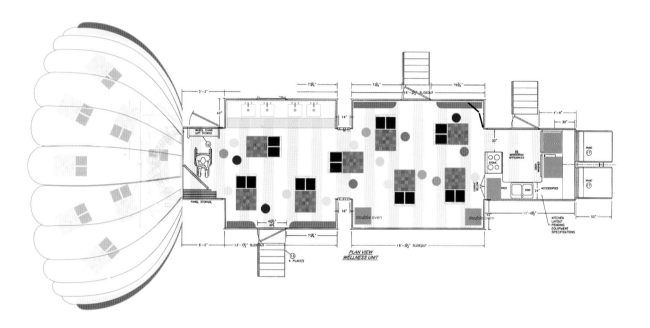

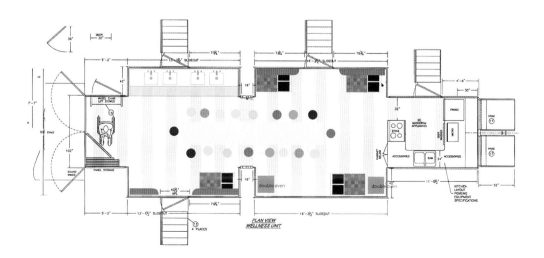

Jamie Oliver's Food Revolution Truck

Jamie Oliver's Food Revolution is a movement to educate kids and families about healthy food. By taking the initiative on the road with a mobile food truck, the Emmy Award–winning chef and his organization, the Jamie Oliver Food Foundation, work to make a greater impact in areas where nutritional education is scarce. When the truck deploys, it hosts an impromptu celebration of the collaboration encouraged by cooking.

The project, which Rockwell Group designed pro bono, is an exercise in using portable design to give greater impact to short-term events. The fully customized 18-wheeler touring truck suggests spontaneity—a nod to Oliver's own style of cooking as well as to the event about to take place. A sunburst of red and white stripes across the body of the truck adds to its vitality.

When it reaches its destination (a school, a street fair, a farmers' market), the truck explodes into a dynamic cooking venue designed to give its students an immediate connection with food. Its sides pop open, expanding to host events and classes both inside and out. Eight mobile cooking stations are outfitted with butcher blocks, storage space, and two heating elements along with a full set of kitchen equipment. Once the cooking is done, workstations can be arranged in clusters for demonstrations or lined up as a long communal dining table. Outside, an inflatable bandshell becomes an ad-hoc amphitheater for temporary events that bring a sense of performance and engagement to the preparation of a meal.

Above
The Food Revolution Truck brings food education and cooking skills to underserved communities.

Right
Chef Jamie Oliver prepares lunch.

DIFFA
Dining by Design

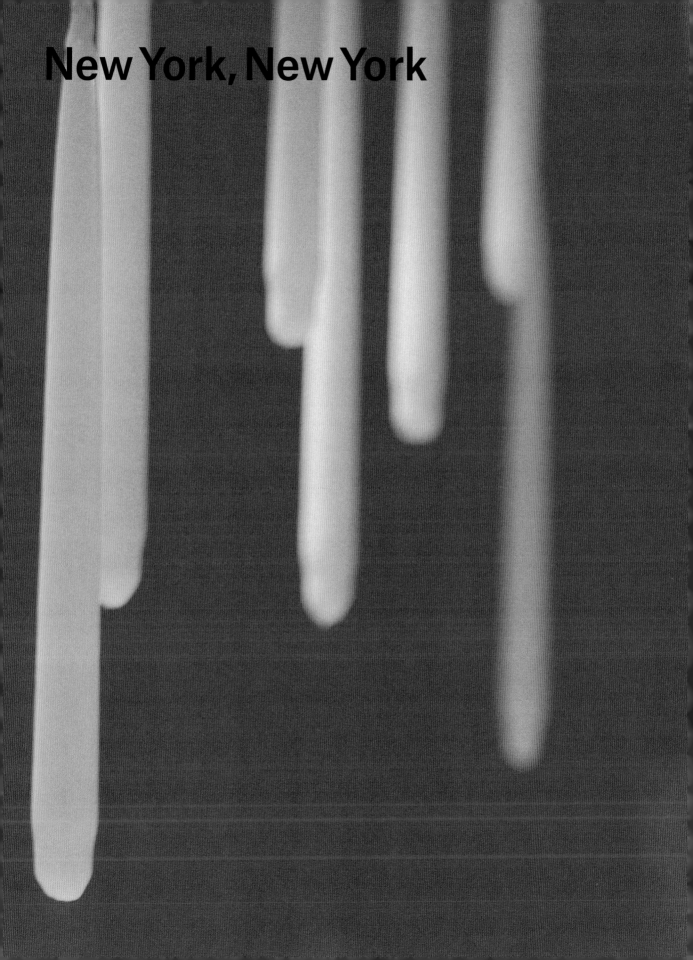

New York, New York

What if the design community donated their talents to raise millions for charity?

I've been involved with DIFFA (Design Industries Foundation Fighting AIDS) since 1994, was its chairman for 12 years, and currently serve as chair emeritus. It's a cause I care about deeply. I lost not only a brother, but also many friends to an epidemic that has profoundly touched the design community. DIFFA gives all kinds of designers, whether they're in fashion, furniture, interiors, architecture, or any related field, the opportunity to use our talents to raise funds for organizations that care for people living with HIV/AIDS or who are otherwise impacted by the disease.

One of DIFFA's most festive moments is the annual Dining by Design fundraiser, where designers go all out to make the most innovative tables. It's always inspiring to see some of the world's most creative minds at work on these fantastic, one-of-a-kind dining environments. And every year the tables seem to get more spirited and inventive. DIFFA's Dining by Design is a testament to the power of the organization in that so many talented people come together to craft these experiences. It's a vehicle for us to celebrate life in the face of loss.

Preceding page
At the 2007 dinner, a 22-foot-long glowing wall was the backdrop for a table that doubled as a place to both cook and dine.

Top
In 2011, flowers that might ordinarily act as a centerpiece were given a new role.

Above
With its ten-foot-tall film screen and glamorous crystal curtain, the 2010 table was inspired by a love of Hollywood.

Right, top
In 2008, guests in this immersive knit environment and ongoing performance could activate integrated LED and sound components.

Right
Conceived as a spalike dining experience, the 2006 installation featured a table surrounded by water.

Untitled at the Whitney

New York, New York

What if a restaurant could vanish at a moment's notice?

One similarity between restaurants and theater is that they don't last forever. Untitled is the first restaurant in a permanent home that is truly demountable. All of the furniture and fixtures, from the simple white-oak tables and room dividers to the seating with red felt upholstery, are packable and portable to quickly transform the restaurant. We wanted the environment to be an understated complement to Marcel Breuer's architecture. This restaurant was not about making a bold design statement; it was about honoring a landmark by creating a comfortable and streamlined space that would harmonize with its midcentury modern elegance.

Flexible mounts allow tabletops to flip vertically.

Cords and electrical outlets are hidden inside hollow room dividers.

Custom cases make for efficient packing.

The Whitney Museum of American Art's landmark granite building, designed by Marcel Breuer, has housed one of the world's most notable collections of American art since its opening in 1966. Untitled is a Danny Meyer–owned restaurant located in the cellar level of the building—except when it isn't.

Designed to be broken down, packed up, and rolled out of the space in just a half hour, the entire restaurant can disappear to make way for museum events. Almost like a theater stage, the 1,500-square-foot area has flexibility that allows the museum to use it as anything from a lecture hall to an auxiliary exhibition space.

But the restaurant is more than a disappearing act. Designed in collaboration with Meyer's Union Square Hospitality Group, Untitled also preserves the authenticity of Breuer's minimal stone-and-concrete architecture with clean-lined white-oak benches, room dividers, and tables whose brushed stainless-steel bases fold flat. Likewise, gray and red wool felt upholstery is similar to 1960s-era textiles, and the restaurant's soffit is embedded with chrome-plated light bulbs that echo the iconic lamps Breuer designed for the museum's lobby. An uptown take on a traditional diner atmosphere, the space also features a large bar area backed by a chalkboard detailing daily specials—which, like the space itself, can be wiped clean at a moment's notice.

Preceding spread
A view of the restaurant from outside Marcel Breuer's iconic granite building.

Left
The restaurant expands to fill the lower level of the museum.

Chairs are durable and stackable.

West Lobby at
The Cosmopolitan

Las Vegas, Nevada

What if no two visits were the same?

Learning from Las Vegas, written in 1972 by Robert Venturi, Denise Scott Brown, and Steven Izenour, was a call to architects to rethink self-aggrandizing monuments in favor of things that appeal to a broader audience. I felt the lobby at The Cosmopolitan was an opportunity to do something more freewheeling and experiential, which is how the city was when *Learning from Las Vegas* was published. People go to Las Vegas for an experience they're not going to get in their hometowns. This was a chance to create a place that would transform every time you visit.

Our LAB developed an experiment with technology that is interactive and responds to visitors as they move through the space. Some of the visual content in the lobby changes very slowly, like the seasons. Some of it alters quite quickly, like the dance that happens from column to column. It's a space people want to come into. Technology doesn't replace the physical environment, it enhances it.

The West Lobby of The Cosmopolitan of Las Vegas was an opportunity for Rockwell Group's LAB to develop technology that would create a new type of visual experience for hotel guests. The LAB envisioned the cavernous lobby as an ever-changing space that would transport visitors from the cacophony of the Strip into a carefully choreographed environment. For this system, 384 frameless LCD screens were installed behind two-way mirrors on each of the lobby's eight structural columns. When the displays are on, images float on the glass; when off, the columns reflect surrounding activity.

The LAB used a prototype of Spacebrew, their open-source environmental choreography software, to make the installation interactive.

Motion sensors convert movement into self-generating patterns that change as visitors traverse the space. Content sequences are keyed to the season or time of day, cycling through falling rain, petals, drifting snowflakes, and *The Dance*, an electrifying video produced in collaboration with choreographer Jerry Mitchell.

Preceding spread
A moment in *The Dance*

Left, top
The movement of visitors through the lobby affects the speed and location of falling snow.

Left
Computer-generated bubbles gently float to the tops of the columns.

6:42 AM

12:15 PM

4:55 PM

8:36 PM

TED Theater

Vancouver, British Columbia

What if a pop-up theater for visionary ideas could be both intimate and grand?

The TED conference is a unique combination of theater and festival, and both are core to a lot of the thinking in our studio. With TED's move to Vancouver, we were tasked with creating, from scratch, a theater designed for the purpose of delivering talks. No one has designed a theater made solely for this form of presentation; we had to invent one! Among the challenges was how the audience would sit in the theater: If you're going to spend four or five days in that room, you may want to recline during some talks and lean in during others.

Plus, the theater needed to be designed and built as a kit of parts that can be assembled and installed in a few days, and then disassembled and loaded into storage for reuse. The pleasure and anticipation of the setup is incredibly important. It's a bit like a circus; the spectacle around its arrival is thrilling. And it's the belief that the physical environment was created just for you. Part of us knows deeply that nothing is forever, so acknowledging the specialness of why we're coming together in a physical space, and that every part of it has been built for this moment, elevates the experience of speakers and viewers alike.

Left
The theater structure uses SHERPA connectors and is a showcase of mortise and tenon, notched, lap, and dovetail joints.

Top
Glulam Douglas fir beams are CNC milled, carefully labeled, and assembled onsite.

Above
More than 8,200 structural beams support the theater bowl.

Following spread
Two rotating 30-person crews can assemble the theater in fewer than five days.

The TED2014 conference marked the thirtieth anniversary of the global ideas-sharing event that brings together speakers from countless disciplines to address a wide range of scientific and cultural topics, often through storytelling. This year also saw the conference's relocation to Vancouver, and with the new venue, the Vancouver Convention Centre, in mind, TED's director commissioned Rockwell Group to design and build a temporary theater within the vast hall.

The goal of the pop-up structure was to create intimacy—an intimacy between the audience and the stage, and between audience members themselves in this amphitheater-like space.

Arranged in tiers around the 24-foot-diameter stage, platforms offered the 1,200 attendees 16 varieties of seating, as well as the option to stand at the back and lean on a rail. The seats included sofas and low-slung lounges, some custom made by Steelcase for the venue.

The environment ultimately affected how each talk evolved, fostering audience comfort and in turn allowing speakers to sense an increased connection with their listeners. The theater's rigorous five-day construction schedule, laid out hour by hour, kept the installation crews moving incessantly, which only added to the momentum and spontaneous magic that surrounds the TED conference.

Preceding spread
The theater is disassmebled, stored, and reinstalled each year.

Above
There is no bad seat in the house—none is farther than 80 feet from the stage.

Right
TED director Chris Anderson in conversation with the audience

On Collaboration

Longtime colleagues discuss shared projects and new modes of practice

Elizabeth Diller and David Rockwell

CHEE PEARLMAN On the face of it, you're not the most likely co-conspirators. How did you first connect?

ELIZABETH DILLER Herbert Muschamp [former architecture critic of the *New York Times*] was keen to introduce us. I remember saying, "What do we have in common with David?" Then I thought, okay, Herbert knows us well, and he knew David well. He had an intuition about putting us together. I don't remember the details, but we went to dinner and I got it. From that introduction on, we've had a dialogue.

DAVID ROCKWELL Herbert took a proactive role with architects. Before I had designed anything for the stage, he strongly encouraged me to do theater work. So when Liz, Ric [Scofidio], and I met, we talked a lot about performance. And we talked a lot about our two studios.

CP What are the differences in your approach to architecture?

DR I think what we're more intrigued with is how our studios are similar, even though the output is very different.

ED Yes, we have more in common than people might think. It's about a sensibility we have as principals. We're both fundamentally entrepreneurial, and we're not happy or satisfied with the architect's role in our discipline. So whereas I went into academia and mostly cultural projects,

and David went into theater and hospitality-related projects, there's an approach that we share. Which isn't to say there aren't certain things that David works on that I'd be allergic to, and he probably feels the same about some of what we do! It's kind of the way opposites attract.

DR As architects, we both have no interest in being defined in a box. For us, the pushing at the edges of that box means there's no reticence about total engagement. Whatever we're doing, we're doing it full on. And that's harder as you get more successful. I think we're both discovering that.

CP Success makes your type of practice more challenging?

DR Yes, it's harder to commit to exploring and pushing as your studio grows with more people and more responsibility. But we both have a desire to step outside the box and explore. Do you think that's true, Liz?

ED Yes. And cooking up projects is something we do pretty well together.

CP Your first go at that was the Viewing Platform built in response to the 9/11 attacks.

DR The Viewing Platform was a combination of dreaming up an idea and the willingness and ability to take action.

ED Right after 9/11 everyone was pretty raw, and I think we were

responding viscerally to the need to bear witness—which was impossible because the entire Ground Zero site was barricaded.

DR The city first brought up the idea of having a VIP viewing platform, and our response was, we won't do that. But we would do a public viewing platform that would let people witness the site in an unmediated way. There was basically no funding available from the city, so with another partner, Kevin Kennon, we created a not-for-profit and raised the money to build it.

ED And we somehow always manage to do it guerrilla style. It has to do with naïveté, and maybe that's the other thing that we have in common, because if we double-checked ourselves, we would have never bothered to do any of these things.

CP It sounds like you were acting as citizen architects.

DR Yes, we realized that this was a real need. It was an emotional need that the city had, and that the world had. It was not really about architecture. In fact, the more the architecture could get out of the way of the experience, the better.

ED We were asking ourselves how simple the Viewing Platform could be, because we had to do it fast. It was like a doctor, going in to help. We felt we had a professional and civic duty to perform.

CP What did you learn about each other through this experience?

ED Well, I thought David was pretty incredible. He was able to get a kind of structure around this project to make it happen. There were all kinds of machinations and hurdles with the city and fundraising that we went through to go from concept to execution in record speed. He was using all his powers, all his contacts and connections, and pulling it all together. It was a big team effort without a client.

DR I learned a lot about trust. I learned to trust the team, and I thought everyone gave freely, and it was amazing how little boundary there was. It was about the ability to just join together to make something happen, and not worry about failing. I don't think any of us looked at the possibility of failure.

CP How have you taken this mode of practice to your current work with Culture Shed?

DR This is also a project that comes from a real need in the city. It didn't start with a typical request for an architectural proposal. It began as a request for ideas for a nonprofit cultural facility in the new Hudson Yards development on Manhattan's West Side. In our early brainstorming, we were both daunted by the question of whether New York really needed another cultural institution.

ED We felt there was a cultural project to be done there, but what could we put on the table that doesn't already exist? So we proposed an institution that would be a cultural hub that could morph and change throughout the year. It would take on different identities in support of the many cultural institutions that are looking for a platform.

CP What is the concept for Culture Shed?

ED We came up with the telescoping sheds right at the beginning. We realized that what New York does not have is a *Kunsthalle*, a brand-free space for showing lots of different things of all different media, and which isn't encumbered the way almost every museum is.

DR But the site actually wasn't big enough to do that.

ED Right. But there was public space there, and we said, wouldn't it be great to be able to temporarily deploy, if we had some kind of telescoping building.

DR And if we could have this transformer type of arrangement, then there may be ways to support vastly different groups who wanted to use the space. And then it was easy to come up with a long list of big events that could take place in New York.

ED And actually, that's where the idea really stems from. If we could shift the paradigm, and make it such that this new institution would actually have to earn its keep, it would be financially independent. How could it do that? With a structure that produces more space when it needs to.

DR It's a flexible space that can transform from a temperature-controlled building with museum-like galleries into an open-air pavilion that can host temporary events like farmers' markets, concerts, large-scale installations, and more.

ED We feel comfortable with the high-low condition, with the commercial/non-commercial, and the profit/nonprofit aspect of this that is not usually part of a cultural program. It's the blurring that's attractive to us.

CP So to close the loop between the Viewing Platform and Culture Shed, is this the basis of a new kind of practice?

ED We've been completely entrepreneurial on both of these. For both we just jumped off a cliff and decided that they had to be done.

DR And by reaching out to a broad group of potential users and key players in the city we've cast a wide net to learn how different people would use the building. Getting a lot of input is a huge part of this kind of initiative. We have to be flexible and respond.

CP It's not often that you see collaborations between offices.

ED Collaboration in this way is very different, because we're cooking up an idea, and we're seeing it happen, and we're controlling its fate. We're nursing it like parents, so we both care deeply about the fate of these projects.

DR This model is based on many levels of trust and experience that we're bringing to the partnership from our respective studios. It's a bit like theater, an intense collaboration that takes place in real time, which is not how architects typically work.

Preceding spread, top
World Trade Center Viewing Platform designed by Rockwell Group, Kevin Kennon Architects, and Diller Scofidio + Renfro

Preceding spread, bottom
Culture Shed's industrial crane technology enables a 16,000-square-foot shed to expand and accommodate different types of events and audiences.

Selected Projects

Cruise Line

Disney Cruise Line: Disney Dream	2011	Worldwide
Royal Caribbean Cruise Lines	2011	Worldwide
Disney Cruise Line: Disney Fantasy	2012	Worldwide

Education

P.S. 6 Library	2004	New York, NY
Robin Hood Foundation: The L!BRARY Initiative—P.S. 17, P.S. 105, P.S. 106, P.S. 137, P.S. 145	2004	Brooklyn, NY
Blue School	2011	New York, NY
Cornell TECH	2013	New York, NY
Columbia University Faculty Club	2015	New York, NY

Event

DIFFA Dining by Design	1997–14 **	New York, NY
Citymeals-on-Wheels Chef's Tribute	2001–14 **	New York, NY
Absolut "Find Your Flavor" Suite	2006	Las Vegas, NV
Bon Appétit Supper Club and Café	2006	New York, NY
Swarovski: Crystallized Oasis	2006	Las Vegas, NV
Public Theater Gala	2008	New York, NY
NBC News/National Education Summit	2010	New York, NY
Jamie Oliver's Food Revolution Truck	2011	Nationwide
SuperFly Presents: The Great GoogaMooga	2012	New York, NY
The Art of Lincoln Center Tableau	2013	New York, NY

Healthcare

Children's Hospital at Montefiore	2001	Bronx, NY
Helen DeVos Children's Hospital	2003 *	Grand Rapids, MI
Cohen Children's Medical Center	2013	New Hyde Park, NY
Atlantic Health's Center for Well Being	2014	Morristown, NJ

Hotel & Spa

Chambers Hotel	2001	New York, NY
W Union Square	2001	New York, NY
WaterColor Inn	2002	Santa Rosa Beach, FL
Le Méridien Chambers Minneapolis	2006	Minneapolis, MN
Aloft Hotels	2008	Worldwide
Belvedere Hotel	2008	Mykonos, Greece
Canyon Ranch	2008	Miami Beach, FL
Carlton Hotel	2008	New York, NY
The Greenwich Hotel	2008	New York, NY
Se San Diego	2008	San Diego, CA
St. Francis Hotel Lobby & Clock Bar	2008	San Francisco, CA
Virgin Spa at Naitar	2008	Peapack, NJ
Ames Boston Hotel	2009	Boston, MA
Ink 48	2009	New York, NY
W Retreat & Spa—Vieques Island	2009	Vieques, Puerto Rico
Andaz Wall Street	2010	New York, NY
The Cosmopolitan of Las Vegas	2010	Las Vegas, NV
Yotel	2011	New York, NY
Le Méridien Oran	2012	Oran, Algeria
The Ritz-Carlton, South Beach	2012	Miami Beach, FL
The Roundhouse at Beacon Falls	2012	Beacon, NY
Secrets The Vine	2012	Cancun, Mexico
W Downtown, Residential Lobby	2012	New York, NY
W Paris Opéra	2012	Paris, France
W Singapore—Sentosa Cove	2012	Sentosa Island, Singapore
Westin Palace Rotunda	2012	Madrid, Spain

Andaz Maui at Wailea	2013	Maui, HI
Nobu Hotel Restaurant and Lounge Caesars Palace	2013	Las Vegas, NV
Fairmont Le Château Frontenac	2014	Quebec City, QC
Grand InterContinental Seoul Parnas	2014	Seoul, South Korea
Hyatt Playa del Carmen	2014	Playa del Carmen, Mexico
Kempinski Munich, Vier Jahreszeiten	2014	Munich, Germany
MGM Grand Hotel	2014 *	Chengdu, China
Nobu Hotel at City of Dreams Manila	2014	Manila, Philippines
Nobu Hotel Riyadh	2014	Riyadh, Saudi Arabia
The Ritz-Carlton Georgetown	2014	Washington, DC
The Ritz-Carlton, Washington, DC	2014	Washington, DC
The Taj Mahal Palace & Tower Hotel	2014	Mumbai, India
Virgin Hotel	2014	Chicago, IL
Yanqi Lake Kempinski Hotel Beijing, Villas	2014	Beijing, China
Abu Dhabi EDITION	2015	Abu Dhabi, UAE
Kempinski Chengdu	2015	Chengdu, China
Margaritaville Hotel	2015	Hollywood, FL
New York EDITION	2015	New York, NY
Nobu Hotel and Restaurant at the Eden Roc	2015	Miami, FL
Nobu Hotel and Restaurant Chicago	2015	Chicago, IL
The Ritz-Carlton, Boston Common	2015	Boston, MA
Time Hotel	2015	New York, NY
Charlotte Marriott City Center	2016	Charlotte, NC
Kioichoi Prince Hotel Tokyo	2016	Tokyo, Japan
Trump Hotel Rio de Janeiro	2016	Rio de Janeiro, Brazil
W Suzhou	2016	Suzhou, China

Interactive

Sheraton Centre Toronto Hotel Lobby Interactive	2007	Toronto, ON
Hall of Fragments, Venice Architecture Biennale	2008	Venice, Italy
Metropolitan Home Design 100	2009	New York, NY
Taste of New York	2009	New York, NY
Plug-in-Play, San Jose Biennial	2010	San Jose, CA
West Lobby at The Cosmopolitan of Las Vegas	2010	Las Vegas, NV
Whitney Museum of American Art's Whitney Shows Off	2010	New York, NY
Timberland Interactive Prototype	2011	Lisbon, Portugal
Google Experience Center, Google Mountain View	2012	Mountain View, CA
Google YouTube, San Bruno Center	2012	San Bruno, CA
INTEL Make Your World Booth, Maker Faire	2012	San Francisco, CA
Time Warner Center Media Lab	2012 *	New York, NY
Google Cultural Institute	2013	Paris, France
INTEL CES Booth	2013–14	Las Vegas, NV
Interactive Virtual Aquarium at Cohen Children's Medical Center	2013	New Hyde Park, NY
Architectural Digest Greenroom at the Academy Awards	2014	Los Angeles, CA

Mixed-use

Mohegan Sun Casino	1996, 2001, 2008, 2009	Uncasville, CT
Millennium Dome	2002 *	London, UK
Seminole Paradise	2004 *	Hollywood, FL
Old Convention Center Master Plan	2007 *	Washington DC
Covent Garden Estate Concept Design	2008 *	London, UK
JetBlue, JFK International Airport	2008	Queens, NY
Marina Bay Sands Casino	2010	Marina Bay, Singapore
Fundadores	2011 *	Monterrey, Mexico
Juana Manso	2011	Buenos Aires, Argentina
Pier 57 Master Plan	2012	New York, NY
Equinox 42nd Street	2014	New York, NY
Horton Plaza	2014	San Diego, CA
City Point Market	2015	Brooklyn, NY

Museum / Exhibition Design

The Declaration of Independence Road Trip	2002	Salt Lake City, UT
Motown Center	2003 *	Detroit, MI
Ertegun Jazz Hall of Fame	2004	New York, NY
Federal Hall Visitor Center	2006	New York, NY
Reinventing the Globe at the National Building Museum	2007	Washington, DC
The Walt Disney Family Museum	2009	San Francisco, CA

Moroso Traveling Show	2011	Nationwide
PLAY WORK BUILD at the National Building Museum	2012	Washington, DC
National Center for Civil and Human Rights	2014	Atlanta, GA
Illuminarium	2015	Worldwide

Nightclub

Cherry Nightclub	2006	Las Vegas, NV
Chandelier Bar at The Cosmopolitan of Las Vegas	2010	Las Vegas, NV
Marquee at The Cosmopolitan of Las Vegas	2010	Las Vegas, NV
Catwalk Bar at VIE Hotel	2013	Bangkok, Thailand
SOCIAL at the Palms	2013	Las Vegas, NV
TAO Downtown	2013	New York, NY
Shang Lounge, Shangri-La at The Fort	2014	Manila, Philippines
Pure Nightclub	2015	Las Vegas, NV

Office

McCann Erickson	2001	New York, NY
Foote Cone Belding	2004	New York, NY
NeueHouse	2013	New York, NY
China Trust Headquarters, Taipei	2015	Taipei, Taiwan

Product

Coke Cruiser	2004	Nationwide
Blue Man Group Product Development	2006 *	Las Vegas, NV
Mikasa Shareware and Barware Collections	2006, 2007	Nationwide
David Rockwell for Dennis Miller Gold Grain Collection	2007	Nationwide
David Rockwell Emeco Chair	2007 *	Nationwide
David Rockwell Collection for Leucos	2007, 2008	Worldwide
David Rockwell for Maya Romanoff Wallcovering Collection	2007, 2009, 2013	Worldwide
Candy Collection by David Rockwell for DESIRON	2009	Nationwide
Saloni Ceramica Tile Collection	2009	Worldwide
David Rockwell Collection for The Rug Company	2010	Worldwide
Imagination Playground in a Box	2010	Worldwide
Rockwell Group for Lualdi Door Collection	2010	Worldwide
Imagination Playground in a Cart	2011	Worldwide
Spotlight Collection by David Rockwell for Jim Thompson	2012	Worldwide
Layered Luxe Collection by David Rockwell and Shaw Hospitality Group	2013	Worldwide
Natural Curiosities Collection by David Rockwell and Shaw Hospitality Group	2014	Worldwide
Caliber Grill by David Rockwell	2015	Worldwide
Lighting & Hotel Accessories Collection for Gaia & Gino	2015	Worldwide

Public Works

World Trade Center Viewing Platform	2001	New York, NY
East River Park	2002 *	New York, NY
Imagination Playground at Burling Slip	2010	New York, NY
B&B Carousell Pavilion at Steeplechase Plaza	2013	Coney Island, NY
Kaufman Astoria Studios Gates	2013	Astoria, NY
Imagination Playground at Betsy Head	2014	Brooklyn, NY

Residential

The Tate	2003	New York, NY
2 Gold Street	2005	New York, NY
96th & 3rd Residential Tower	2006	New York, NY
Octagon Park Apartments	2006	New York, NY
50 Biscayne Blvd	2007	Miami, FL
Riverhouse	2007	New York, NY
75 Wall Street	2009	New York, NY
15 Central Park West Residence	2010	New York, NY
One MiMA Tower	2011	New York, NY
East 58th Street Residence	2012	New York, NY
House Beautiful Designer Visions Showhouse Apartment	2012	New York, NY
Apogee Beach	2013	Hollywood, FL
Capitol Place	2014	Washington, DC
222 East 40th Street	2015	New York, NY
Brickell Heights	2015	Miami, FL

The Viceroy at Snowmass	2015	Snowmass, CO
101 Murray Street	2016	New York, NY
Tower D at Hudson Yards in collaboration with Diller Scofidio + Renfro	2017	New York, NY

Restaurant & Bar

Django	2002	New York, NY
Strip House	2002, 2007	Livingston, NJ / Las Vegas, NV / Naples, FL / San Juan, Puerto Rico
El Vez	2003, 2014	Philadelphia, PA / New York, NY
Emeril's	2003	Atlanta, GA / Miami, FL
Red Lounge	2003	Chicago, IL / Los Angeles, CA
Rosa Mexicano	2003, 2005, 2006	Washington, DC / New York, NY / Atlanta, GA
Sushi Samba	2003	Chicago, IL
Twenty Four Fifth	2003	New York, NY
Café Gray, Time Warner Center	2004	New York, NY
Kittichai	2004	New York, NY
Mesa Grill at Caesars Palace	2004	Las Vegas, NV
Nectar	2004	Berwyn, PA
Washington Square Restaurant	2004	Philadelphia, PA
Bar Americain	2005	New York, NY
Café at Country	2005	New York, NY
Country	2005	New York, NY
Maze	2005	London, UK
Nobu 57	2005	New York, NY
Nobu Dallas	2005	Dallas, TX
The Ramp at Club Med	2005	Punta Cana, Mexico
Bobby Flay Steak	2006	Atlantic City, NJ
BRGR	2006	New York, NY
Nobu Atlantis	2006	Paradise Island, Bahamas
Nobu Hong Kong	2007	Hong Kong, China
Nobu Melbourne	2007	Melbourne, Australia
Nobu San Diego	2007	San Diego, CA
Nobu Waikiki	2007	Honolulu, HI
St. Honore Bakery	2007	New York, NY
Adour Alain Ducasse	2008	New York, NY
Adour at The St. Regis Washington, DC	2008	Washington, DC
BLT Burger at the Mirage	2008	Las Vegas, NV
Blue Ginger	2008	Wellesley, MA
Dos Caminos	2008	Las Vegas, NV
J & G Steakhouse	2008	Scottsdale, AZ
Matsuhisa Athens	2008–9	Athens, Greece
Nobu Dubai	2008	Dubai, UAE
Nobu Los Angeles	2008	Los Angeles, CA
Payard Patisserie & Bistro at Caesars Palace	2008	Las Vegas, NV
Simon at Palms Place	2008	Las Vegas, NV
Wildwood BBQ	2008	New York, NY
Yellowtail	2008	Las Vegas, NV
A Voce Columbus	2009	New York, NY
Bar Americain at Mohegan Sun Casino	2009	Uncasville, CT
Bobby's Burger Palace	2009	Multiple Locations
Harbour Bar at the Taj Mahal Palace Hotel	2009	Mumbai, India
Maialino	2009	New York, NY
Matsuhisa Mykonos	2009	Mykonos, Greece
Nobu Mexico City	2009	Mexico City, Mexico
Nobu Moscow	2009	Moscow, Russia
Wasabi by Morimoto at the Taj Mahal Palace Hotel	2009	Mumbai, India
Jaleo at The Cosmopolitan of Las Vegas	2010	Las Vegas, NV
Nobu Budapest	2010	Budapest, Hungary
Real Sports Bar & Grill	2010	Ottawa, ON
Todd English P.U.B.	2010	Las Vegas, NV
E11even	2011	Toronto, ON
Nobu Beijing	2011	Beijing, China
Silver	2011	Park City, Utah
Talon Club at The Cosmopolitan of Las Vegas	2011	Las Vegas, NV
Untitled at The Whitney	2011	New York, NY
Wolfgang Puck at Hotel Bel-Air	2011	Los Angeles, CA
Astor Grill at The St. Regis Doha	2012	Doha, Qatar
Gordon Ramsay Doha	2012	Doha, Qatar

The Library at The Public Theatre	2012	New York, NY
Ritz-Carlton New York, Central Park South	2012	New York, NY
The Smith	2012	New York, NY
Sugar and Plumm	2012	New York, NY
Argo Tea	2013	Multiple Locations
Creative Juice	2013	Multiple Locations
Decanter at St. Regis	2013	Washington, DC
Ellary's Greens	2013	New York, NY
Five50 at ARIA Resort & Casino	2013	Las Vegas, NV
Morimoto at Andaz Maui at Wailea	2013	Maui, HI
Todd English P.U.B.	2013	Birmingham, AL
Travelle at The Langham, Chicago	2013	Chicago, IL
Yellow Tail Sushi Bar at VIE Hotel	2013	Bangkok, Thailand
Chef's Club	2014	New York, NY
Gato	2014	New York, NY
Nobu Doha	2014	Doha, Qatar
Lambeau Field Restaurant	2015	Green Bay, WI

Retail

Champs Flagship Store: 5 Times Square	2002	New York, NY
Meijer	2003	Grand Rapids, MI
FAO Schwarz	2004	New York, NY
Central Department Store	2006 *	Calcutta, India
Crossroads	2006 *	Mumbai, India
Forth & Towne	2006	West Nyack, NY
Mikasa Store	2006	Stamford, CT
Dubai Exhibition City Plaza	2008 *	Dubai, UAE
Mauboussin Flagship Store	2008	New York, NY
Crystals at CityCenter	2009	Las Vegas, NV
Harry & David	2010	Nationwide
Bangkok Fitness Concept	2013	Bangkok, Thailand
Bloomingdales	2013	Glendale, CA
Not Your Daughter's Jeans, Bloomingdales	2013	New York, NY
Shinola Flagship Tribeca	2013	New York, NY
Jim Thompson Showroom	2014	Atlanta, GA

Set Design

Hairspray	2002	New York, NY / National Tour
Omnium Gatherum	2003	New York, NY
Team America: World Police	2004	Los Angeles, CA
All Shook Up	2005	New York, NY
Dirty Rotten Scoundrels	2005	New York, NY
Armed and Naked in America, Off-Broadway	2007	New York, NY
Legally Blonde: The Musical	2007, 2009	New York, NY / London, UK
Let Me Down Easy	2008	New Haven, CT
Catch Me If You Can	2009, 2011	Seattle, WA / New York, NY
Peep Show	2009	Las Vegas, NV
81st Academy Awards	2009	Los Angeles, CA
82nd Academy Awards	2010	Los Angeles, CA
ELF	2010	New York, NY
A Free Man of Color	2010	New York, NY
Little Doc	2010	New York, NY
The Normal Heart	2011	New York, NY
CQ/CX	2012	New York, NY
Dead Accounts	2012	New York, NY
Harvey	2012	New York, NY
Kinky Boots	2013	Chicago, IL / New York, NY
Lucky Guy	2013	New York, NY
Power of Duff	2013	New York, NY
SIDE SHOW	2013	La Jolla, CA / Washington, DC
Carmen	2014	Houston, TX
Houdini	2016	New York, NY

Sports

NFL Los Angeles Hacienda	2003 *	Los Angeles, CA
Meadowlands Stadium, Club & Suites	2010	Rutherford, NJ
Green Bay Packers Hall of Fame	2015	Green Bay, WI

Strategy / Branding

Asbury Park Boardwalk	2006 *	Asbury Park, NJ
Disney—Future Reports	2009	Worldwide
7 for All Mankind	2010	Los Angeles, CA
Outback Steakhouse	2010	Nationwide
North Face	2011	Nationwide
Lucy Activewear Store Redesign	2012	Nationwide
Marriott International—Future of Meetings	2014	Worldwide
All Aboard Florida	2016	Miami, FL

Theater / Performance Venue

New Amsterdam Theater	2002 *	New York, NY
The Incubator Project in collaboration with Kevin Kennon Architects	2004 *	New York, NY
ArtsQuest/SteelStax Cultural Center	2005 *	Bethlehem, PA
Bangkok Theater at Siam Paragon	2005	Bangkok, Thailand
Cirque du Soleil	2005 *	Hong Kong, China
Nokia Theatre Times Square	2005	New York, NY
Phantom of the Opera, Venetian Hotel	2006	Las Vegas, NV
Elinor Bunin Munroe Film Center	2011	New York, NY
Mega Bangna Cineplex Bangkok	2012	Bangkok, Thailand
Hat Yai, Chiang Mai and Ubon Theaters	2013	Bangkok, Thailand
Rangsit and Embassy Movieplexes	2014	Bangkok, Thailand
Southampton Center for the Arts	2014 *	Southampton, NY
TED Theater	2014	Vancouver, BC
Resorts World Manila Theater	2016	Manila, Philippines
Culture Shed in collaboration with Diller Scofidio + Renfro	2018	New York, NY

* Concept
** Ongoing

Acknowledgments

This book has been an incredible journey through our firm's work over the last ten years and an exciting moment to reconnect with the talented people we've collaborated with along the way. I have many to thank, but first want to express my sincere appreciation to everyone at the Rockwell Group. The spirit and energy of the team has created an environment of curiosity and creativity that inspires me every day.

My deep gratitude goes to Marc Hacker, the driving force behind this project, for his invaluable wisdom, leadership, and generosity of spirit. And I thank Chee Pearlman, a trusted advisor who has brought her considerable editorial talent and vision to the making of this book. I am grateful to Shannon Harvey for her strategic eye and attention to detail at every turn, to Adam Michaels and Anna Rieger of Project Projects for their phenomenal work on the book's concept and design, to Molly Heintz for her work in shaping the early storylines, and to Diana Murphy at Metropolis Books for her wonderful enthusiasm and editorial guidance.

Additional thanks to Joan MacKeith and her marketing and communications team for their incredible work in positioning everything we do, and to the other company leaders who drive Rockwell Group forward: Carmen Aguilar, Vin Cipolla, Dawn Condon, Diego Gronda, Melissa Hoffman, Greg Keffer, Barry Richards, LeAnn Shelton, Nina Stern, Shawn Sullivan, Chuck Wood, and David Yanks.

I would also like to acknowledge those who contributed to the book in many different ways: Lauren Adams, Blaine Alexander, J. T. Bachman, Zachary Boka, Beth Bowles, Claire Bryant, Evelyn Choi, Patrick Dierker, Michael Etzel, Jordan Farkas, Michael Fischer, Yulia Frumkin, Erin Gouveia, T. J. Greenway, Dick Jaris, Patty Johnson, Caroline Kim, Lena Kim, Melissa Klein, Gail Kutac, Tai-Li Lee, Max Mensching, Andrea Monfried, Claire Myers, Joanna Neborsky, Donna Pallotta, Meghna Pathak, Sheela Pawar, Brett Renfer, Michael Sean, Melinda Sekela, Siji Small, James Tichenor, Branden Torres, Gerry Vyhmeister, Joshua Walton, Olivia Witte, and David Zaccheo.

A heartfelt thanks to my lifelong friend and advisor Henry Edwards.

And finally, to Marcia, Sam, and Lola, who every day encourage me to ask "What if...?" and teach me the importance of love.

About the Contributors

David Rockwell is an award-winning architect and designer. He is the founder and CEO of Rockwell Group, based in New York, with satellite offices in Madrid and Shanghai.

Justin Davidson is a Pulitzer Prize–winning classical music and architecture critic for *New York Magazine*.

Elizabeth Diller is a founder of the inter-disciplinary design studio Diller Scofidio + Renfro, and is a professor of architecture at Princeton University.

John Guare is a Tony Award–winning playwright and screenplay writer.

Jack O'Brien is a Tony Award–winning director, producer, writer, and lyricist.

Chee Pearlman is a curator, editor, and conference director specializing in design and architecture.

Managing editor: Shannon Harvey
Design: Project Projects
Project director, Metropolis Books: Diana Murphy
Contributing writer: Jennifer Krichels
Copyeditor: Mary Christian
Research and permissions: Alie Cirgenski,
Emily Rinaldi

Separations and printing: Oceanic Graphic
International, Hong Kong, China

Library of Congress Cataloging-in-Publication
Data is available upon request.
ISBN 978-1-938922-56-5

Metropolis Books
ARTBOOK | D.A.P.
155 Sixth Avenue, 2nd floor
New York, N.Y. 10013
tel 212 627 1999
fax 212 627 9484
www.artbook.com
www.metropolisbooks.com

METROPOLIS BOOKS